Dial 9

IF YOU ARE FED UP WITH LIMI-
TATIONS AND ARTIFICIAL BAR-
RIERS—the technique works. Sydney
Omarr's method for predicting future
courses of action and interpreting unconscious desires and thoughts have
helped people in all walks of life—
artists, poets, film stars, psychiatrists,
hypnotists, speculators, and athletes—
gain insight into matters of love, business, and friendship. They have testified that THE THOUGHT DIAL WAY
has brought forth astounding results.

"Omarr has had an amazing record of accuracy
in his astrological analysis. He is the only man
who has ever been assigned by the armed
forces to fulltime duty as an astrologer."
—*Glendale News-Press*

"AN ABSOLUTELY FASCINATING
BOOK."
—*Oklahoma City Oklahoman*

D1330064

For Expanding Your Personal Knowledge of
Astrology, SIGNET Brings to You
SYDNEY OMARR'S
WEEKLY ASTROLOGICAL GUIDE
FOR YOU IN 1973

ARIES	P5098	LIBRA	P5104
TAURUS	P5099	SCORPIO	P5105
GEMINI	P5100	SAGITTARIUS	P5106
CANCER	P5101	CAPRICORN	P5107
LEO	P5102	AQUARIUS	P5108
VIRGO	P5103	PISCES	P5109

(60¢ each)

Also from SIGNET

SYDNEY OMARR'S ASTROLOGY GUIDE FOR TEENAGERS
(#P4225—60¢)

SYDNEY OMARR'S ASTROLOGY GUIDE TO SEX AND LOVE
(#T4249—75¢)

The Thought Dial Way To A Healthy And Successful Life

by
SYDNEY OMARR

With an introduction by
Carl Payne Tobey

A STUART L. DANIELS BOOK

A SIGNET BOOK from
NEW AMERICAN LIBRARY
TIMES MIRROR

SIGNET TRADEMARK REG. U.S. PAT. OFF. AND FOREIGN COUNTRIES
REGISTERED TRADEMARK—MARCA REGISTRADA
HECHO EN CHICAGO, U.S.A.

SIGNET, SIGNET CLASSICS, SIGNETTE, MENTOR AND PLUME BOOKS
are published by The New American Library, Inc.,
1301 Avenue of the Americas, New York, New York 10019

FIRST PRINTING, FEBRUARY, 1973

PRINTED IN THE UNITED STATES OF AMERICA

CONTENTS

PART THREE

The Thought Dial Explanation

The original hardcover *Thought Dial* went through seven editions before being published in paperback. Then came the enlarged, new-dimensional *Thought Dial Way to a Healthy and Successful Life*, which broke down barriers and opened a door to exciting experimentation, including the section, *Thought Dial as Time Machine*. It is this large, new book, new-dimensional and challenging, which we have here in paperback and it is this book which I want to discuss briefly and explain.

Most important, we have here a potential "time machine," a way of "dialing our time," of creating conditions we want, need, desire or require. This aspect, this newest dimension, this *time machine concept*, is fully explained in the chapter, "Thought Dial as Time Machine." And it is the time machine utilization which I want to clarify here, in this New American Library edition. As stated in early chapters, the *actual dial* is not necessary for utilization of *Thought Dial*. The key is to come up with numbers spontaneously selected, off the top of your head, as it were. The dial is a convenience, an apparatus, a mantram, a physical device, but is not absolutely necessary for the operational principles of *Thought Dial*. Give three numbers and give them *spontaneously*; that is the ticket. Refer to the cover for this. Do indulge, though, in ordering a dial (see the back of this book) for your complete convenience.

Now, as for "setting the dial" on a single number, as in the time machine section and concept: READ AND ABSORB THE ENTIRE SECTION. WHEN YOU HAVE DECIDED WHAT KIND OF TIME IT IS YOU WANT TO ATTRACT, PLACE YOUR FINGER ON THAT NUMBER ON THE COVER HERE (WHEN YOU GET YOUR DIAL, USE IT, OF COURSE). RELAX AND VISUALIZE THE EVENTS AND TIME WHICH THE NUMBER SYMBOLIZES. Your subconscious will do the rest. CAUTION: *Take care with what you request because you are going to get it.*

In other, more conventional uses of the Thought Dial technique, such as Answering Direct Questions, Tapping the Subconscious, Locating Lost Articles, Picking Winners, etc., merely place a finger at the "start here" point and move your finger *spontaneously* and in any direction to three numbers. (Move the hand of the dial when you have that.) This means *any three numbers*, and you also may repeat a number. Then you merely add and arrive at a single digit, as explained.

The technique works. Results are obtained. People in all walks of life, from Aldous Huxley and Henry Miller to Jayne Mansfield and Marjorie Main to the proverbial man-in-the-street, have worked and successfully utilized the *Thought Dial*. Psychiatrists and hypnotists, artists and poets, speculators and athletes, all are included in a gallery of individuals who have testified, by letters, calls, in print and in person, on radio and television (from Art Linkletter to Johnny Carson) that *Thought Dial* is fun, "nontoxic" and can bring forth astounding results.

—Sydney Omarr
March, 1972
Santa Monica, California

Acknowledgments

I would like, first of all, to acknowledge a debt of gratitude, long due, to Carl Payne Tobey, president of the Institute of Abstract Science at Tucson, Arizona. It was Mr. Tobey, an excellent mathematician, astrologer and writer, who first encouraged me to continue work on the *Thought Dial,* who offered the facilities of his organization at Tucson, and who published the first review of this work in his excellent *Student Forum.*

It was many years ago in New York that I first encountered Tobey. I was then publishing *Astrology News,* the trade journal of astrology. It was the first such publication in the field. Like all firsts, it was not always easy going. Among those who supported the young man brash enough to step in where older, wiser men feared to tread were Carl Payne Tobey and Llewellyn George, the publisher.

The late Mr. George was one of the finest gentlemen to be found anywhere, in or out of astrology. And there were others who foresaw the need of a journalistic approach to the vast field of astrology, persons who lent moral and financial support. Though *Astrology News* is no longer issued, its influence is still being felt in modern astrology, where today it is no longer unusual for publications to report in a concise, objective manner, on what astrologers are writing, doing and thinking, and also what the field, in general, is doing to better its sorely neglected concept of public relations.

As mentioned, there were a number of persons who, through their initial support of the trade paper, can claim credit for this healthy trend. Ralph Schaeffer of New York was one. The Church of Light, in Los Angeles, was another. Dorothea and Robert De Luce, also of Los Angeles, were most enthusiastic, and in the same city The Self-Realization Fellowship was a regular advertiser. The individuals who came forward make up a who's who of astrology and include Nona Howard of Boston, Blanca Holmes of Los Angeles, Ernest Grant of Washington, D.C., Charles Luntz of St. Louis, Edward Wagner of New York, Marc Edmund Jones, the late Elbert Benjamine, Doris Chase Doane, Florence Campbell and Clifford Cheasley.

All this, perhaps, has nothing to do with *Thought Dial*. Not on the surface, anyway. But the experience with *Astrology News* convinced me that those who engage in the study of astrology are practicing a universal language, one which is destined, as it was in the past, to be spoken with greater regularity.

It was Tobey who, with his knowledge of mathematics, was able to comprehend the idea of *thoughts through numbers*. He was sure that the Thought Dial represented a valuable contribution to workers in the fields of psychology and astrology. His enthusiasm has never wavered.

Like Tobey, I feel we have in the Thought Dial a key to a better understanding of numerical and planetary symbols, and through these symbols, an added key to the mysteries of the subconscious mind. I believe that the subconscious, just as it does in dreams, attempts to make itself heard via these symbols.

I have earned something of a reputation for reliability in the fields of news and astrology. It is a reputation I value. I gladly stake it on *Thought Dial*.

—Sydney Omarr
Los Angeles

Introduction

by Carl Payne Tobey

President, Institute of Abstract Science

In order to explain the Thought Dial, it would be necessary to explain the mind, and no one has done a very good job of that yet. Explanations have been attempted by theologians, philosophers and psychiatrists, but none of these explanations have been very ingenious. Educators regard it as a vacuum into which you pour something. Biologists think it is a bunch of cells in the brain. Freud placed it nearer the sex organs.

Because educators look upon the mind as a vacuum into which you pour something, it is seldom realized that all truth originally came out of the mind of someone. The greatest truths are abstract truths. When we point to an object and say it is a tree, this does not involve any kind of truth. It has merely to do with man's idiotic habit of classifying everything into groups. The great abstract truths are mathematical truths, theorems, etc. All of man's progress and all real science is based on such abstract truths. These truths came out of the minds of men. Truth is something that exists in an abstract form, and were it not possible for us to contact it, there would be no known mathematical theorems. Without these, there could be no science. The only true science is mathematics. It is pure abstraction. Other so-called sciences are largely hoaxes, for they are merely a matter of classifying things according to some predetermined arrangement.

Mathematical truths are discovered when they come into the mind of someone. The history of mathematics shows that mathematicians often awaken out of sleep with

some great truth in their minds, or they dream a mathematical theorem. It comes to them in a dream. Churches,
schools, colleges and universities leave us with the impression that truths are found in textbooks. When statistical
principles were first employed to prove the existence of
extrasensory perception, precognition and clairvoyance,
John J. O'Neill, late science editor of the New York
Herald Tribune, wrote that science had just discovered
what everybody had always known.

Phenomena like "clairvoyance" were recognized long
before science ever investigated them. People talked about
second sight, but over a long interval anyone able to bring
forth truth from the abstract in such a manner was
regarded as a witch and an agent of the devil. Churches
and other social institutions had various methods of
dealing with witches. In the western-desert part of our
own country, where water is scarce and water-dowsers are
relied upon by ranchers and banks, the term "water
witch" is still prevalent.

It was not too long ago that only women believed in
intuition. The first statistical tests conducted by Dr. J. B.
Rhine of Duke University demonstrated that one out of
five persons, on the average, has some amount of extrasensory perception. One of the principal reasons why
the other four do not have it is because they have been
taught not to have it by our strange educational system.
They have been taught that there is no such factor. They
have been taught to ignore their intuition and their
hunches and stick to the doctrine of materialism.

Back in 1938, I was one of the persons who took the
extrasensory-perception tests at Duke University, as given
by the late Dr. Charles Stuart, mathematician and expert
in this field at that time. I proved to be one of those four
who showed no signs of extrasensory perception. I left
Duke with several decks of the extrasensory-perception
test cards, and headed to Florida, where I began making
tests on many people. I made a few observations of my
own. I noted that my best subjects were people born
during the interval of each year when the Sun is in
Sagittarius. I noted that people who could not score above
normal usually guessed the *first card correctly*. This factor
was later investigated at Duke, with similar results. I also
noted that, in my own case, when there were but five
symbols to guess from, I could picture all five symbols at

once. This seemed a handicap. With others, I observed that relaxation of a subject had much to do with correct guessing. I conducted an experiment of my own with myself as a subject.

I used an ordinary deck of playing cards and had to guess a specific card with the odds 51 to 1 against me. After the cards were carefully shuffled and cut, they were put away on a table until sometime within the next 24 hours I had an involuntary impression of a card from the deck. When this happened, the card was written down and then checked against the top card on the deck. I succeeded in guessing the first five cards correctly. If this was due to chance, it was against odds of 380,204,031 to 1.

In later years, I tried using such faculties for discovering mathematical formulas. I discovered the prime number *dendrite* which mathematicians had sought unsuccessfully for 2,500 years. All I did was relax and reflect on the problem after retiring at night. On the third night, I had the answer.

I am convinced that actually *all knowledge* of any subject is within your own mind at all times, because it is there in the *abstract*. The problem is to bring it forth. There is an abstract world. You have contact with that world if you wish to exercise it. In the abstract world, there is no time and no space. You can only have time when there is change. Nothing ever changes in the abstract world. Any mathematical theorem is the same today as it was in the time of Euclid and Pythagoras in 500 B.C. The great mathematicians, who have been the greatest of all scientists, have been men who were able to contact the abstract world. You need have no insecurity when dealing with the abstract world because you need never fear that anything in it will ever change. The whole study of the abstract world comes under the heading of mathematics. Mathematics deals only with the abstract. Its application in the material world is something else again. Even astrology is actually a study of the abstract, and therefore is a form of mathematics. Perhaps the best branch of mathematics to study, to learn to see what the abstract world is like, is *Number Theory,* originally given birth by the mathematician Pierre de Fermat. In 500 B.C., Pythagoras was seeking something similar in *numerology*. Perhaps Fermat was one of our best examples of a man who was able to contact the abstract world and write down what he saw there. He discovered a vast number of new mathematical theorems.

The abstract world is a world of design. It is beautiful design. All great mathematicians have seen the abstract world as a world of beauty and have described it as such. Our educators do not teach us to see into the abstract world. They merely teach us to memorize what others have recorded from that world, or to know where to look it up in a book of formulas. When you can do this, you are not necessarily a mathematician, but you may be an engineer. Engineers apply the mathematical knowledge that others have brought back from the abstract.

A true conception of the word "intellect" would involve that part of the mind with which we may contact the abstract world. *We stand in a balance between the intellectual and the emotional worlds.* The emotions have their own purposes, but they cut us off from the abstract and prevent our use of the intellect. To contact the abstract, we have to walk away from the emotional. You almost have to be alone to contact the abstract through the intellect. Society is an emotional organism. When you follow society, you have little chance of contacting the abstract. You have to cut yourself away from society. You contact the abstract best when you learn to be alone, completely independent and immune to what others may think about anything. Even our religions belong mainly to the emotional rather than to the intellectual world. There is no devil in the abstract world. He is a product of the imagination we find in the emotional religious world. Yet, when the theologian speaks of the Will of God, he is seeking the abstract world, for the abstract world is the Will of God. It is the Word.

The laws that govern the universe are abstract laws. Physical laws are actually abstract, although material obeys them. Sir Isaac Newton, who discovered the laws of gravitation, saw them not as any force, but as abstract mathematical law. The laws of planetary motion are abstract mathematical laws discovered by the astronomer Johannes Kepler. No astronomers can explain why all free bodies in space travel in ellipses rather than in circles. They just do. They obey a mathematical law.

Now, what is the Thought Dial of Sydney Omarr?

When you want to know the correct time, you can dial a number on your telephone and get the right answer, all automatically. In a way, the Thought Dial operates in somewhat the same manner. At least it has for the writer on numerous occasions. It has turned up with the right answers in some manner.

You may have a question on your mind. It may be a very serious question. Probably the more serious the better. You dial a number and zip comes the answer. To say the least, it is remarkable. *It is almost as if you were telephoning some master of all wisdom within yourself.* He sees all and tells all. This is just the writer's reaction to what he has seen, but it would seem that Omarr has devised a means of bypassing the conscious and getting into the unconscious. I won't say the subconscious, because I think it may involve the superconscious. I think the superconscious mind contains a super calculating device that makes all electronic calculators look like simplicity itself. I know there is such a device because I have often employed it in mathematical work. I too have awakened in the night with the answer to a very complicated mathematical problem clearly before me. This takes practice and relaxation, but Omarr seems to have a means of going to less trouble. He appears to bypass the conscious in the same or similar manner to that in which the conscious is bypassed in hypnotism. The function may not be too unlike the individual who prays for divine guidance and gets it. There are many people who do not believe this can be accomplished, never try it and so never get divine guidance. Perhaps the Thought Dial is a means of achieving this goal.

If the Thought Dial is unorthodox, then to hell with orthodoxy. We have been taught enough clap-trap by orthodoxy. You can never be an intellectual until you toss orthodoxy and all of its superstitions out the window. Much that has been taught as science is pure superstition. A large part of astronomy is mere superstition. A large part of what has been taught as religion is superstition. We will meet the true science and the true religion as one and the same thing in the abstract mathematical world. The Thought Dial deals with numbers. Frankly, I do not know whether it has anything to do with numbers and their actual characteristics as studied in Number Theory, or whether the numbers actually apply only as a part of some code between the conscious and the unconscious. I do know that numbers have characteristics and that no two numbers have exactly the same characteristics. Anyone who understands Number Theory knows that. Numbers are all a part of that great cosmic and abstract design, and everything that ever happens in the universe happens only in accord with the abstract design.

Perhaps the Thought Dial is a means of contacting the abstract.

It seems appropriate that *Thought Dial* should be published when men are reexamining their moth-eaten educational system in order to see what changes are going to be necessary in the era of space travel. You can use *Thought Dial* as something that is entertaining, or you can take it more seriously. Perhaps it will set you to thinking. Perhaps it will help you to learn more about the human mind—your mind. Perhaps it will help to open up some of the unlimited possibilities of mind that have been hidden from us by so much false science and so much false religion. Try it out. See what it does for you.

People often joke about looking into a crystal ball to see what the future holds. They joke about it because they can't see what the future would be doing in a crystal ball. It isn't there. The crystal is merely a means to an end. It is a means of fixing the conscious attention on a point and allowing the unconscious to take over. In this way, some form of contact with the abstract appears to take place for some people. You might not be able to see anything in a crystal ball. Most people can't. A materialist could smash a crystal to bits and prove to his own satisfaction that there is no future in a crystal ball, but materialists have never heard of that factor we call mind. They cannot deal nor cope with what they do not know exists.

A great many people are unable to adjust their subjective world to the objective world. Because of the condition of the subjective world, they are seldom able to truly explore the reality of the objective world. There are many such persons in mental institutions, and far more outside of mental institutions. Some of them may be housewives. Others are teaching in schools and universities. It is unfortunate that under our educational system such people are often given the responsibility of handling our young, when instead they should be receiving treatment. I have no desire to fool myself, and when first confronted with the Thought Dial, I was on guard against this very thing. Over a period of years, it always worked for me. Would it work for others? Would it work for everybody or just for some people? This is not an easy thing to find out. We can't answer for everybody, because we don't know everybody, and we can't test everybody.

The truth is always within yourself, if you could only bring it out, but there are a lot of things other than the truth that are also hidden in your subconscious. There is a very ancient saying that first thoughts are best. This has some basis in fact, and it has been proved in extrasensory-perception tests that most people will be likely to guess right the first time. The second guess is not as accurate as the first. There may be some connection. The Thought Dial is a way of guessing when you are unconscious of doing so. You ask for numbers, and your subconscious tosses them up from somewhere. They come up in such a way that they have value *when applied to the* Thought Dial. It is a strange phenomenon, but most interesting. It stimulates one's curiosity, and all progress in the world has occurred because someone became curious. Otherwise, life would probably develop into a dull routine. The Thought Dial will help keep life from becoming monotonous. It's fun, but it's a lot more than that. It holds the answer to some of the many mysteries of the mind. Get curious and do a little exploring. Try it out on your friends. Help them with their problems. Be a very careful observer. See whether you can find a case where it doesn't work, and if you do, report the case with great care. The nearest thing the writer had to a negative report was from a person who wrote, "It doesn't get into my subconscious. *It tells me exactly what I'm thinking about consciously*, and it does it all the time." Well, even that is rather odd!

Society, the victim of mistaken teachings in the realms of religion and science, has been slow to penetrate to the truth of the mind and its possibilities. Despite evidence produced in various universities pointing to the existence of extrasensory perception, there remains a large body of psychologists who reject the idea of an "extra sense." One such group declared it could not accept ESP in spite of the evidence because it was too contrary to *ordinary* concepts. That statement is best understood if we examine the meaning of the word "ordinary"; one dictionary definition, for example, is "inferior." The school of thought that cannot let go of the concept that mind is subservient to matter is, however, losing ground. Publishers are not bound by it. Astronauts have reportedly been instructed in the possible utilization of ESP if they should be cut off from all other means of communication in space. Many nations, including the Soviet Union, are investigating ESP.

An astrophysicist from the California Institute of Technology puts forth some interesting observations relative to our conventional modes of thinking. Dr. Fritz Zwicky, in his *Morphological Astronomy,* draws a parallel between the way people think and rain falling on the earth, running down mountainsides, through valleys to the sea. The rain uncovers a little of what is beneath the surface, but once it has established its watercourses, most of what is below remains hidden. The ruts and gullies that are formed determine the paths of future floods. Yet, when a river occasionally gets off its course it may reveal a buried city, an important mineral deposit or other information and material of immense value. Dr. Zwicky points out, however, that it is in the nature of most people to dig ever deeper into their ruts, but without carrying away the debris as do the waters. Instead, people throw the debris up and over the edge, making more certain that it will be impossible to see anywhere but within the rut they are in; they throw the debris into the eyes of neighbors, blinding them, too.

There are predetermined valleys of *thought,* just as there are well-established stream patterns. Dr. Zwicky maintains that if we knew more about these valleys of thought we would be able to determine more easily the direction in which to search for new truths.

Sydney Omarr is gifted with an uncanny knowledge of the paths to truth. In some manner his intuitive knowledge penetrated those predetermined valleys of the ancient past when he created *Thought Dial.*

In the middle-1940s a youthful Sydney Omarr strode into my New York office. I was eager to meet him because his work in journalistic astrology had intrigued me. He then edited and published astrology's first and only trade journal, *Astrology News.* His articles, when they appeared in such leading astrological journals as *American Astrology* and *Horoscope,* were free of the usual clichés. They were stimulating and cut through the deadwood that had so long weighed down astrological literature. While I had wanted very much to meet Omarr he chose an unpropitious time to call. I was feeling gloomy and was reluctant to betray my concern. Sydney, then in his twenties, studied me for a moment. He asked me to do something that struck me as rather questionable: *he asked me for three numbers*. Although preoccupied with my personal concerns and somewhat skeptical, I complied. Then without warning my interest was aroused and I had the eerie feeling that my mind was an open book to the tall, quiet young man before me.

He said, "You are concerned by what you consider the beginning of a relationship."

That was true enough, and now I was staring, wondering how that connected with the three numbers I had at random mentioned. But Omarr said, "Stop being bothered. The relationship you think is beginning has already ended."

Now I wasn't so sure about the brilliance I had previously attributed to this young man. How could something be finished when it had just begun? And how could he even know something had started, when only I knew—along with the other party involved?

But Omarr seemed undaunted, even slightly amused by my perplexed expression. He went on to tell me, in a straightforward manner, "Forget about this specific question. Put it in the past, because the relationship has ended."

Indeed this was a very strange thing for Omarr to say, because I had just helped someone to finance a new business. I was concerned, even worried. But Omarr, on the basis of three spontaneous numbers I had given, was telling me that the matter was finished. I didn't see how it was possible.

More than twenty years have passed and not once since that time have I seen the person who so occupied my thoughts that day. Of course, I had no way of knowing then how accurate Omarr's forecast would prove to be. But somehow I did know that this lad was worth listening to. He had already probed many unorthodox subjects. He was an Army Air Corps veteran and at one time had been given full-time duty as an astrologer, conducting a program for Armed Forces Radio Service. He wanted to write a book telling people about thinking by analyzing a series of numbers given at random. And he wanted to call it *Thought Dial*. Omarr did what he said he wanted to do—and the rest is history.

Let me tell you some more about my experience with Omarr, probably one of the best-known men in the art of bringing astrology, number symbolism and other border-line areas out of the clouds and down to earth, where all can intelligently utilize them.

Approximately two years ago I was talking over the long-distance telephone to Bill McGaw, editor and publisher of the *Southwesterner,* a journal on the Old West. For some reason McGaw brought up Sydney Omarr. He asked whether I knew him. I said I did.

"Well," said McGaw, "when I was a sportswriter with the old Philadelphia *Record,* a boy no more than fifteen or sixteen called me. I found out how old he was because I met him a couple of months later. But when he called I thought he was off base, far out. You see, Carl, he claimed he could pick the winners of prize fights if I could get him the birth dates of the boxers."

"Did you?" I asked. I knew Omarr was a Philadelphian and much interested in boxing.

"Yes," McGaw replied, chuckling. "What started out as a gag turned into quite a mystery. That kid, claiming he was using astrology and numbers, picked the winners in 23 out of 25 boxing matches!"

I believe that Sydney Omarr is one of those persons possessing inexplicable powers of the mind. Over a period of years this opinion has been strengthened by events. I once noted an odd circumstance. I would decide to telephone him in Hollywood from my home in Tucson on some matter, but I would first try to finish a task at hand. In that interval my phone would ring and Omarr would be on the other end of the line. Recently a matter came up which made it imperative for me to discuss a situation with Omarr. I decided to call, but then the phone rang. It was Omarr, who asked, "What do you want? I got a message from you—a strong one."

A few days later I related this incident to a group of radio and television people who had assembled at my house. One lady, scoffing slightly, said, "All right. Let's all concentrate on Sydney Omarr and see if we can get him to call." Within five minutes the phone rang. I answered it. Omarr dispelled the lady's skepticism.

On another occasion, while visiting Omarr in Hollywood, I was relating an experience that had occurred back in the 1920s. We had just returned from a fine dinner with interesting friends. I was disturbed because I could not remember the name of a lady who figured prominently in the anecdote I was relating. I went on with the story, without the name. When I had finished I complained, "I wish I could remember her name."

Suddenly Omarr held up his hand for silence. I watched and listened as *he began to spell out the name* I hadn't been able to remember.

Noticing my startled expression, he explained, "That name just came into my mind. It didn't mean anything to me, but I just wondered whether it might be the name of the woman you couldn't remember."

It was—but where did he get that name? Did he draw it out of my unconscious? Did he draw it out of some cosmic memory? *The events in the story I had been relating had occurred six years before Sydney Omarr was born!*

Extrasensory perception involves various phases of mental phenomena including intuition, psychic powers, mental telepathy, precognition (memory in reverse), hunches, etc. The original Thought Dial appeared to involve a method of digging into the unconscious and bringing forth information concealed from the conscious mind. The new Thought Dial (which Omarr likens to a "time machine") has a new dimension, an added something that would appear to be more closely related to *psychokinetics*. This involves one's ability to influence people and objects at a distance. The parapsychologists have apparently demonstrated that the enthusiastic dice-thrower, one who "coaxes" the dice, gets better results than the individual who just tosses and trusts to chance. The player who "talks" to and "commands" the cubes comes up with the right numbers more often, often enough to exceed the laws of chance. This seems to be akin to Omarr's time-machine concept, "ordering" the subconscious by feeding it a number symbol.

One way we can learn much more about these subjects is to stop sweeping evidence under a rug by calling it "coincidence." The late Charles Fort asked, "What if it shouldn't be coincidence?" Nobody has ever bothered to answer that question, probably because no one can.

There is some strange something in the unconscious that will do what you tell it to do if you know how to give the orders. Down through the centuries, there have been those who have tried to keep all such knowledge from the rank-and-file. In the realm of astrology, the truth of the ancients has been twisted and distorted. Being a mathematician I am conscious of that fact.

I am also aware that at least one person (if not hundreds) reading these words will say something like, "Okay, I'm ordering my subconscious to go out and rob a bank and bring me the money!" He will be a very unhappy individual. It will not occur to him to first seek happiness. At this moment I think of a man who had accumulated hundreds of millions of dollars. He spent the last year of his life grousing because, according to him, nobody loved him. You may wonder why I inject that story here. I'll tell you why. When you work the Thought Dial, be cautious.

Watch out that you don't dial the wrong number!

Carl Payne Tobey
Tucson, Arizona

Part ONE

1

The Basic Principles of Thought Dial

The Thought Dial, although it can be utilized as a game for fun and amusement, is much more than a toy. It is an instrument based on sound psychological principles, especially those enunciated by the renowned Swiss psychologist Dr. Carl G. Jung. Jung, in his work *The Interpretation of Nature and the Psyche* (1955), used the word "synchronicity" which he explained as the simultaneous occurrence of a certain psychic state with one or more external events which appear as meaningful parallels to the momentary subjective state.

Jung made use of the term to describe a coincidence. He never asserted that coincidental events of whatever nature necessarily stemmed from the same cause. Students of astrology should find this easy to comprehend, especially those who have studied the writings of Carl Payne Tobey, who maintains that events that appear to coincide with planetary positions and aspects are not representative of causal phenomena. Rather, says Tobey, astrology is a form of abstract mathematical expression.

Perhaps the Thought Dial can best be compared to horary astrology, in which a question, thought or idea is presumed to be "born" and a chart is set up for the moment of birth, as if the question, thought or idea was a human being for whom a horoscope was being cast.

23

The Thought Dial represents, in one sense, *horary astrology with numbers.*

The Thought Dial implements Jung's principle of synchronicity, to the extent that a thought, a question or idea is reduced or defined into a number and planetary symbol.

The Thought Dial is a valid, *mantic* procedure for tapping the subconscious. Thoughts, like everything else in nature, find expression through numbers. As Pythagoras said, "Nature geometrizes."

Jung declared, "Since the remotest times men have used numbers to express meaningful coincidences . . . those that can be interpreted."

The celebrated Dr. Jung displayed far more courage and originality than many of his colleagues. He overcame fear of academic prejudice. He was not afraid to speak out on such subjects as extrasensory perception, the mystery of numbers, astrology and psychic phenomena. His findings lend support to the principles behind the Thought Dial. Jung's studies show that numbers and planets are effective keys to analyzing character, perceiving thoughts and foretelling the future.

Many scientists agree with Jung about "occult" subjects. However, lacking his reputation, they hesitate to express themselves in public. That is why Jung is mentioned repeatedly here as a reference. But students who are familiar with my previous works know very well that a number of outstanding thinkers have long been intrigued with the vast possibilities such a study as this represents. Jung asserted that a sequence of numbers is more than a mere stringing together of identical units. He said that numbers and synchronicity have always been brought into connection with each other. *Mystery* is a common characteristic of both.

Number, perhaps more than anything else, brings order out of apparent chaos. To quote Jung again: "It [number] is the predestined instrument for creating order, or for apprehending an already existing, but still unknown, regular arrangement. . . ."

He says, too, that number perhaps is the most primitive element of order in the human mind: "Hence it is not such an audacious conclusion after all if we define number psychologically as an *archetype of* order which has become conscious." (Italics mine.)

Now, upon first experimentation with the Thought Dial, a natural objection might arise: "But, after all, I don't know what the numbers mean. So how can my conscious or subconscious mind express itself through numerical symbols?"

Once more, let us turn to Jung. He presents the possibility that numbers are *not*, as is commonly thought, inventions of the conscious mind of man. Instead, they are *spontaneous* productions of the unconscious. Jung asserts that "it follows irrefutably that the unconscious uses number as an ordering factor."

Jung repeatedly stresses the possibility that numbers were *found or discovered*. If this is true, and Jung was inclined to believe it was, numbers would have the characteristic or quality of being, in his words, *pre-existent to consciousness*.

It can be presumed, at least as a working theory, that the subconscious is familiar with the number symbols and what they represent. The unconscious mind, or the subconscious, or the superconscious, races past the conscious, or the *censor*, in expressing itself via these symbols.

Tradition, experimentation and experience are the components making up the number interpretations. Experience, for example, has taught that the number 6 represents domesticity, concern with matters affecting the home. Often a change of residence coincides with subconscious expression totaling 6. That digit is (via the same components) associated with the planet symbol of Venus, which in its turn represents a zodiacal symbol and area associated with various aspects of character, thought and events.

The subconscious or hidden, mind, presumed to be familiar with these symbols and their associations, brings them forth to the conscious area through utilization of the Thought Dial.

Basically, therefore, the Thought Dial operates on ancient and modern concepts of astrology and numerology, and it extends these into the modern field of psychology, as valid in its way as any other psychological testing device. Dr. Jung, indeed, declared that "Astrology represents the summation of all the psychological knowledge of antiquity."

Astrology is, like everything else, closely associated with

number. The Thought Dial, combining number and planet symbols, bypasses the conscious "censor" mind and probes deep, shaking hands with the truth that inhabits us all.

2

What the Dial Numbers Symbolize

Number ONE: the beginning; it is birth and life, independence of both thought and action. It is a time for the new, for the launching of projects. This digit is associated with the Sun.

Number TWO: a force that is emotional and negative rather than direct and positive. It is symbolic of diplomacy, a time for tact, for caution. The number is associated with the Moon.

Number THREE: a relief of pressure, symbolic of humor and versatility. It is a time for getting out of a rut. However, a scattering of forces must be avoided. The temptation is to try to do too much at one time. Three is associated with Jupiter.

Number FOUR: the square; it is routine and hard work and the handling of details. There is strength here, but only if creative thought or imagination is brought into play. This is a time to slow down. The number is associated with Uranus.

Number FIVE: change and travel, the creative arts, relations with members of the opposite sex, speculation—these are stressed. Communication of ideas becomes a necessity. Your personal magnetism increases. Five is associated with the planet Mercury.

Number SIX: emphasis is on the home, change of residence, the rediscovering of loved ones. Diplomacy is a requirement here, just as with the number 2, only in a larger sense. The digit is associated with Venus.

Number SEVEN: self-deception; the tendency is to confuse the ideal with the real. Not a time to enter into legal pacts. An aura of illusion dominates. Seven is associated with the planet Neptune.

Number EIGHT: a time for pushing ahead vigorously. The symbols of this number are power, strength, marriage and reproduction, ardent pursuit of business goals. The number is associated with Saturn.

Number NINE: is completion, the end of a cycle, a time to finish projects. Avoid new starts, be wary of new contacts. Often indicates the bearing of another's responsibility. Universal appeal, wide publicity also shown. Nine is associated with Mars.

Number ELEVEN: a master digit. Stress is on intuition, teaching. Hunches are to be trusted here. The influence is far-reaching; it is a time for expressing ideas, no matter how radical. The number is associated with Uranus.

Number TWENTY-TWO: also a master digit. Emphasis is on building, creating, making master plans. Must not be bogged down with detail or influenced by persons with no vision. Twenty-two is associated with the planet Pluto.

3

Numbers as Objects

It was Gertrude Stein who, perhaps more than any other person in modern times, treated words as "objects." She believed that each word was an entity; she became fascinated with words for the life within them, for the "vibrations" or meanings they expressed. Miss Stein sometimes became so enamored of the words as *separate* objects that she deliberately overlooked meanings as a *whole*. She was, in this sense, a writer's writer. The general reading public, often unaware of her meaning, sometimes found her puzzling. But her influence has prevailed. Her mark is to be found in some of the best of modern works. In effect, she was the conductor of a noble experiment. She took hold of the language and shook life back into it. Those she influenced, such as Ernest Hemingway, Thornton Wilder, Sherwood Anderson and Richard Wright, were forever in her debt and were celebrated by the same people who found it fashionable to smirk at her "words as objects." She conducted numerous experiments in so-called automatic writing under the tutorship of the famed philosopher and psychologist William James. Words had become objects to her, similar to numbers, and often *denoted* by number.

All this is by way of introducing the notion of numbers as objects, as forces or influences; the number 1, for example, standing as a beacon to the new, to independence, to originality, to innovation. Number 1, like all numbers, is one thing as a *symbol*, and quite another when taken alone as a number, or utilitarian object to be part of the operation involved in adding or subtracting, multiplying or dividing.

In this sense, mathematicians and numerologists are much closer to agreement than astronomers and astrologers. Astronomers are largely involved with the dimensions and orbits of planets and stars. So far as planets as symbols or influences on human affairs are concerned, they remain woefully ignorant, or stubborn, or both.

With mathematicians, the story is different. Mathematicians are more familiar with numbers than astronomers are with planets. This fact becomes obvious after only the most superficial examination. I, for one, can testify to the obstinacy of astronomers. I have debated with at least three leading astronomers on astrology. Each claimed, before the debates, to know the subject. After the debates, however, each admitted he had little or no knowledge of astrology. Why, then, did they debate in the first place? That question, in itself, would require a psychological study. The astronomers, generally, have a fixed, *erroneous* concept of astrology. When their views are exposed to the light of public debate, this fact is forcibly driven home.

The late Pulitzer Prize winner John J. O'Neil, then science editor of the New York *Herald Tribune*, wrote me, after my debate with Dr. Roy K. Marshal, former director of the Fels Planetarium, that such attacks on astrology should be regarded as symptoms of professional paranoia. These incidents are related here because astrology, or the symbols utilized in the subject, combine with numbers to make the Thought Dial an instrument of value.

Number 1, through tradition and experiment, is associated with the Sun, which in turn is related to the zodiacal sign of Leo the Lion. So the digit, although it denotes independence, is also related to thoughts, things and events associated with the Sun and with Leo. Taking Aries as the natural first sign of the zodiac, Leo becomes the fifth sign or house, associated with affairs of the heart, speculation, adventure, children. Leo rules the heart and back and is strongly connected, also, with entertainment and with creative forces, from sex to artistic expression. Leo is the showman, as the most elementary student of the zodiac can testify.

There are a number of systems of house division in astrology. I am using a traditional one, the one that associates Leo with the fifth house. *But it is not the only one.* Mr. Tobey, after painstaking and brilliant research placed Leo at the forefront of the first house. His revolutionary and iconoclastic work has contributed much to astrology. But the vast majority of experiments conducted with the Thought Dial involved the so-called traditional method, making Aries the natural first-house indicator, Taurus the second, Gemini the third, Cancer the fourth, Leo the fifth, and so on down the line, to Pisces as the twelfth house.

I believe that through further experiments *a combination* of the Tobey system and the traditional one, as used here, will prove of immense value. For example, in the Tobey system, Leo is a first-house sign. Leo is associated with the Sun in both methods. And, though Leo is traditionally a fifth-house sign, the Sun is associated with number 1, the *first* digit, the beginning, the pioneer, the start, the self-expression.

Leo, though traditionally of fifth-house value, most certainly contains elements of the FIRST, also. The same is true of Cancer. In traditional methods, Cancer is the fourth house. Tobey places that sign on the cusp of the second house of the natural zodiac. The Moon, which rules Cancer, is number 2. So, *through numbers,* the similarities become more evident than the differences.

The student will soon become aware, as I have pointed out to Tobey and other leading astrologers and number students, that the *house meanings themselves* are too similar to the number symbols for this to be mere coincidence. I believe that the astrological houses gained their meanings from the numbers.

Creative mathematicians are in agreement that numbers indeed are objects containing properties of their own, meanings, symbols, "personalities," even influences of their own. Without number, there wouldn't be very much of anything else, certainly not much of a civilization as we know it today.

As Constance Reid points out, in her excellent book, *From Zero to Infinity,** "number is an abstraction, a recognition of the fact that collections may have something in common even though the elements of the collection have in common nothing whatever." Or, as Bertrand Russell declared, "It must have required many ages to discover that a brace of pheasants and a couple of days were both instances of the number 2." In other words, numbers are objects in themselves, to be studied for individual meanings and properties, and numbers, also, are abstractions, representing, among other things, *symbols of thoughts or ideas*.

This, perhaps, becomes easier to comprehend when we think of words as symbols of our thoughts. It is not only *not* fantastic to think of words as depicting our thoughts, or expressing them, it would be ridiculous to deny that power to words. Thus words are related to numbers, *once the numbers are understood*. Words, through numbers, are easier to understand, as a study of the works of Cheiro, or Ariel Yvonne Taylor, or Florence Campbell, or Clifford Cheasley or other numerologists will reveal. Words, through a simple process, can be transformed to number, each letter containing a numerical value of its own, just as each number contains a letter value, an element (number 4 is an "earth element"), a characteristic, a thought symbol, etc.

Numbers are the objects upon which the Thought Dial is built and upon which, to a large extent, it operates.

Thoughts are abstract expressions made solid (objects) and thus easier to examine and comprehend—through the use of numbers.

The Thought Dial helps make this possible.

* Thomas Y. Crowell Company, New York, 1955.

4

How to Operate
the Thought Dial

Operation of the Thought Dial is simple—that is, as far as the physical movements or operations are concerned. A finger, preferably the forefinger, is placed on the arrow, as indicated. And the arrow is moved to three digits, which are then added and reduced to a single number. *The only double numbers detained as totals are 11 and 22.* That is the simple part.

But there is more to the Thought Dial than the mere physical apparatus, or "going through the motions."

It is important to form a thought clearly, concisely: either in the form of a question, a picture-thought, or through the simple act of relaxing, so your number selections are not hurried. In many cases, the arrow *will move fast*, so fast it will appear to be moving itself. In other instances, the process may resemble a man confined to a torture chamber—everything slow, crawling, nothing definite. When finally you have dialed three numbers, perspiration will stand out on your forehead. Other times, all will be harmony. The arrow indicates three numbers and the total is arrived at—the interpretation given, an answer or solution found. *Actions of the Thought Dial depend upon your state of mind, your thoughts or your questions.*

Remember, the Thought Dial is merely a physical instrument through which you measure and analyze intangibles, such as thoughts, questions, ideas, speculation about the future. The Thought Dial, in your hands, is basically you!

Now, let us confine ourselves to the physical operation of the Thought Dial. First, place the forefinger on the arrow, as indicated. Then, after your thought, idea, or question is formed, or when you are simply relaxed, allow your finger, or the arrow *to carry your finger,* to any three numerical symbols. The start, of course, is made where indicated, from the zero symbol.

The three numbers are then added and reduced to a single digit. The only double numbers retained are 11 and 22.

Suppose, for example, you dial 4 . . . 8 . . . and 6. These numbers total 18.

Number 18 is reduced to a single number by adding from left to right, thus: 1 plus 8 = 9. The Thought Dial total of 4 plus 8 plus 6 is 9.

It is a simple operation. Number 9, in this instance, becomes the symbol of your subconscious thought, or question, or idea—it tells something of the character of your mind or thoughts at the moment, and tells much more, too.

The interpretations are given in the various sections of this book: YOUR SUBCONSCIOUS THOUGHTS, HOW TO LOCATE LOST ARTICLES, YOUR QUESTIONS ANSWERED, THE YES AND NO TECHNIQUE, AND PICKING WINNERS.

But always check the number symbols, so that you become familiar with them, so that you can experiment. Take notes, test the Thought Dial. Let us have your findings.

For example, in this case the total is 9. A check of the section *What the Numbers Symbolize* tells us that number 9 is associated with completion, the end of a cycle. It is a time to finish projects rather than to try new projects. Number 9, it has been found, often is the nurse, the humanitarian: it is a person, too, who carries another's load on his shoulders. It is time to discard the past, to get rid of burdens—to prepare for the future.

Generally, as an indicator of SUBCONSCIOUS THOUGHTS, the number 9 would indicate that one phase of life or activity was drawing to a close, a new one about to begin.

Number 9, in answer to a DIRECT QUESTION, would answer that this was the end of an association, a relationship, a project—the answer would be in terminating a relationship and getting ready to start out with new ideas— a display of independence.

As a symbol for LOCATING LOST OBJECTS, number 9— literally—might mean that a child has the object among some clothing.

In the YES AND NO technique, number 9 would be considered positive, or YES.

In PICKING WINNERS, number 9 would be associated with Mars, and with names of horses or teams or athletes, whose names were similar to Mars-9 relationships, such as: IRON, COMPLETION, ACTION, FIGHTER, WAR LORD, LEADER, INVENTOR, etc.

Each section, of course, contains complete explanations and interpretations.

For now, let us review the basic operation:

1. Relax. Form thought or question clearly in mind.
2. Place forefinger on indicator, which rests at zero position.
3. Continue to concentrate.
4. Move dial, or allow it to move, to any three digits.
5. Total the three numbers.
6. Reduce all double numbers, with the exception of 11 and 22, by adding from left to right.
7. The total is your Thought Dial indicator, the symbol of that particular thought, idea, or question.

NOTE: Dial *any* three numbers, using zero position as a starting point. This does *not* eliminate zero as a number. For example, you could dial 3 . . . 0 . . . 7, which would total 10. When added, 10 would equal 1 plus zero, or 1.

If your total should be zero, which would result if you dialed to zero three times, then you should once more relax, concentrate upon your thought, and start over.

You CAN repeat numbers. For example, you could dial 7 . . . 6 . . . 7.

Allow yourself FREEDOM OF THOUGHT, or motion. You can dial around the circle or not, as you wish or *think*.

That is the physical operation of the Thought Dial. From here on, we will be most concerned with INTERPRETATIONS of totals which result from this operation.

EXAMPLE: Subject dials numbers 22, 8 and 11. These numbers are added:

22 plus 8 plus 11 = 41.

4 plus 1 = 5.

The total of 22, 8 and 11 equals 5.

REPEATING: The only double numbers kept as final totals are 11 and 22! All other numbers are reduced to single digits by adding from left to right.

5

Variations in Dialing

It might be asked why the subject is told to dial three numbers. Why not one? Why not four? Or five? Or any total?

The answer is that my research was based on a series of three digits. The experiments thus far conducted with the Thought Dial have been concerned with the series of three. This is not to say that another total might not be equally as effective. Perhaps, in some instances, the workings of the Thought Dial would be enhanced with a different series.

Thus Sepharial, in discussing thoughts in relation to number, advocates a series of nine numbers, which are then reduced in the usual manner. And to which the number three is added. Sepharial also cites examples of other experts in these matters who take only one number—deriving their interpretation from that single digit.

It is my belief that, if working with the same subject, the operator of the Thought Dial might be well advised to *vary* his technique. Perhaps the subject is working the Thought Dial in a series of tests. Use the three-number method, vary it with the series of nine digits, with the number 3 added to the total. The Thought Dial, like thought itself, is fluid: it is not fixed. Nor is this text intended to be gospel.

The material here, in most instances, is put down as the result of experiments that proved fruitful. The important thing to remember is the Thought Dial is *merely an instrument through which the subconscious mind is permitted to express itself*.

In continuous experiments with a subject, it might be advisable to vary methods of arriving at a total. The significant factor is the *total*, whether that total is arrived at by the dialing of three numbers, or one number, or nine numbers with the addition of three to the final answer.

Example: Operator has subject dial three numbers to obtain insight into his *subconscious thoughts*.

Subject is then requested to think of a *specific question* and to once more dial three numbers.

The subject has yet another direct question. Once more he is instructed to dial three numbers.

Subject, at this point, has a question concerning a *lost article*. Operator requests that he dial *nine* numbers, which are added and reduced in the usual manner—except that number three is added to the total.

Subject, in asking still another direct question, is once more instructed to dial *three numbers*.

In conclusion, subject—in selecting "a winner"—is told to dial *one* number.

By this technique, the subject's interest is held. This is an important point to remember. Dr. Rhine, in his numerous experiments with ESP, concluded that *higher scores* resulted when the subject's interest was at a peak. As the interest waned, so did ESP scores.

Why this is so, I leave to others to determine.

6

Numbers and Thoughts

It is known that, prior to his death, inventor Thomas Alva Edison was hard at work on a so-called Telephone Between Worlds, an instrument through which, Edison hoped, it would be possible to "tune in," or connect, with another world, if there be one—the world of the soul, or personality, or memory, or whatever part of man survived after his bodily death. Whether Edison's device involved numbers, or was in any way similar to the Thought Dial, is not known. This is pointed out to show that wise men—men who have pioneered and invented—men like

Sir William Crookes, Sir Arthur Conan Doyle, Jung, Edison and others like them—have not been afraid to experiment with the abstract. Men like J. B. Rhine have, in effect, "measured thoughts," often doing so in the face of ridicule from colleagues. It is now, of course, possible to measure brain waves. And it is hoped that the Thought Dial will represent at least a start in the direction of "solidifying" thoughts, ideas, mental impulses, insights into the future, etc.

The validity of the Thought Dial, to a large extent, depends upon numbers as symbols—symbols whose meanings are clear to the subconscious mind, or *continuous memory*.

In his work *The Soul of the Universe*,* scientist-astronomer Dr. Gustaf Stromberg declares that the results of his studies are "that the individual memory is probably indestructible. . . ." Dr. Stromberg came to the United States from Sweden in 1916. He was on the scientific research staff of the Mount Wilson Observatory of the Carnegie Institution of Washington from 1917 to 1946. And of his works, Albert Einstein said, "Very few men could of their own knowledge present . . . material as clearly and concisely as he has succeeded in doing."

And it is Dr. Stromberg who asserted, "The memory of an individual is written in indelible script in space and time—it has become an eternal part of a Cosmos in development." Stromberg believed that the brain receives *waves* from a kind of universal brain, or soul. That, in effect, the brain is merely a filtering mechanism, permitting certain ideas and thoughts to flow through from "the soul of the universe."

Of *thoughts,* he says, "In addition to conscious reasoning there exists also a certain type of unconscious reasoning in which people think with their 'feelings,' and sometimes even to better advantage." Stromberg was always cooperative whenever I consulted him. I once arranged for a radio discussion between Stromberg, novelist Aldous Huxley and James Crenshaw, a newspaperman and authority on psychic phenomena. The discussion was of great importance, both for what was said on the air, and statements made off the record.

One thing Stromberg was on the record with was this

---

* David McKay Company, New York, 1941.

statement: ". . . thoughts can be transmitted from one individual to another (telepathy), and there is then no logical reason why they cannot be transmitted from an individual to the Soul of the Universe and from the Soul of the Universe to an individual (inspiration)."

This becomes simpler to comprehend when we conceive of the thoughts as symbols expressed through number. And that, it may be said, is the purpose of the Thought Dial, the combining of numbers and thoughts, the identifying of thoughts and ideas with number symbols.

Now let us put the Thought Dial to use. It can be used personally, for the solution of your own problems. But the professional psychologist, astrologer or student, as well as the hobbyist, can also utilize the Thought Dial in aiding others.

With experience, other uses will be found; but for now the basic sections that follow are headed:

SUBCONSCIOUS THOUGHTS
DIRECT QUESTIONS ANSWERED
YES AND NO TECHNIQUE
LOCATING LOST ARTICLES
PICKING WINNERS

These "other uses" are references to the skill that practice brings. For example, the subject thinks of an individual, dials three numbers. You total the digits and reduce to a single number. Let us suppose it is 7. That number is associated with the planet Neptune, which rules Pisces. You can start out, thus, by stating that the person being "thought about" was born under Pisces, which would be from February 20 to March 21. And the description of the person would fit the Pisces-Neptune-7 characteristics, and so on. And, often, when a person merely dials three numbers, without necessarily concentrating on a problem, he reveals *his own date of birth*. He does this in the manner provided by the above example.

Experience through experiment will unlock the door to other fascinating procedures and possibilities.

7

Your Subconscious Thoughts

In this operation, the subject merely dials three numbers without consciously thinking of a specific question. The idea is to permit the subconscious to come through, past the censor, or conscious mind, as it would through a dream. The "dream," in this instance, is the Thought Dial and the number totals.

Remember, in all instances, the subject dials to three numbers, which are added from left to right and reduced to a single number, the only double numbers retained being 11 and 22.

IF THE TOTAL IS ONE:

The number is the individual, the original, it is a need and subconscious desire for independence of thought and action. Originality is stressed. THE SUBJECT HAS A DESIRE TO GIVE OF HIMSELF THROUGH CREATIVE, ORIGINAL, INDIVIDUAL MEANS.

Number 1 is associated with the Sun, which in turn, rules Leo, the natural fifth zodiacal house. The creative urge here is strong, but not necessarily—in this case—as a need for sex expression. Rather, the subject seeks *new forms of expression*, an original way of presenting an old package.

The old is to be discarded in favor of the new, in favor of the pioneer. The subject is being told by his subconscious: TAKE A CHANCE!

The number 1, as a total on the Thought Dial here, represents new enterprises, a chance to get in on the ground floor, to start from the bottom. It represents a need for courage. A pioneer must work and move in the face of obstacles, the biggest obstacle being the past and so-called tried and true methods.

Most often, with this total representing subconscious

38

thought, the subject is perplexed about whether to go along the same path, or take a sharp turn to a new road. THE ANSWER IS THE NEW.

The Sun (symbol of this digit) will attract attention, but its very brightness draws moths—the human kind who damn with faint praise.

Right now, with the 1 total, the subject has no need for the advice of the stable, well-meaning friends and associates. Number 1 is the Sun with a touch of Uranus, just as 4 is Uranus with a touch of the Sun.

SPECULATE! ACT! CREATE!

Members of the opposite sex, because of the Leo-Fifth-House influence, often represent a barrier here. So do children, responsibilities, etc.

The element here is FIRE. ORIGINATE, LEAD, PUSH THROUGH PROGRESSIVE MEASURES.

Promote yourself! Your subconscious, in effect, pleads with you to be vain, if necessary, but move AHEAD. On your own!

IF THE TOTAL IS TWO:

Number 2 is associated with the Moon: as a subconscious-thought indicator it tells a story of brooding, indecision, worry over the possibility of an abrupt change. This number, as a total on the Thought Dial, stresses the need for DIPLOMACY. The subject is advised to WIN HIS WAY—this rather than resorting to methods of force.

Abrupt decisions, the subconscious is trying to say, should be avoided.

The element of this number is Water. Intuition is stressed. But there is a fine line between intuition and a tendency to make something out of nothing, to worry and brood. Number 2, through its association with the Moon, is also related to the zodiacal sign of Cancer. The tendency here is to collect, to be ultra-sensitive concerning security. But the BEST ADVICE appears to be: SIT TIGHT FOR THE MOMENT.

Number 2, like the digit 6, is the moderator, the diplomat. It will be important for the subject to keep out of triangles. Avoid becoming entangled in battles, controversies. Others will try to involve the subject, will bring him their problems. It would be a mistake, at this time, to take sides. That's the message of the subconscious, as relayed through the Thought Dial.

Avoid weighing yourself down with items which eventually will have to be discarded—that's another significant message to the subject, whose total adds to 2. Be aware of security, but avoid being miserly.

Number 2, although it may seem a symbol of *inaction*, is really similar to a yellow traffic-light signal. Wait, but be ready. Win your way rather than push through by force. Be willing to exercise caution and diplomacy, but do not allow yourself to be squeezed out of the picture. Have patience.

The home is emphasized here. Protection: a valuable ally could appear from your actual home, or near your home, or the ally could be the subject's partner.

The tendency here is to look afar, when actually help may be close by.

Where a 1 total urges action, this digit, 2, advises a waiting game. Wait—but remain alert!

By all means avoid brooding! Others may try to encourage quick decisions. But the subject should review the situation: he would have everything to lose and nothing to gain by impulsive action.

Avoiding impulsive action applies to affairs of the heart, conditions in the home, dealings with older persons, with the parent or parents, with the buying or selling of property.

The subject, through the dialing of this total, should be greatly relieved. The key words are "No news is good news."

IF THE TOTAL IS THREE:

Number 3 is associated with the planet Jupiter; it is a symbol of expansion and humor, as well as good fortune. However, as a total on the Thought Dial, it often relates to confusion. There is a seriousness of purpose which is generally lacking. The tendency, here, is for the subject to try doing too much at one time. Thus the subconscious is warning against a scattering of forces. "One thing at a time," is the obvious message. Number 3, through Jupiter, is related to the zodiacal sign of Sagittarius, and with ninth-house matters, such as long journeys, both physical as well as journeys of the mind, such as philosophy, higher education, etc. It is a number, this 3, of self-improvement, of gaining through a light touch, a sense of fitness or humor.

The element is Fire; as a total, in relation to subconscious thoughts, the digit expresses a joy in living, tells of improved social life, important contacts to be made at parties, gatherings, etc.

Versatility is a keynote here. The subject should not be tied down to any one method, or person, for that matter. There is a tendency, as revealed through the Jupiter symbol, toward extravagance, not only in financial matters, but in affairs of the heart, in the emotions. For example, to overlook details, to forgive others for their errors, no matter how careless. Generous to a fault—that, too, could describe the state of a person whose total is 3.

Number 3, to use an analogy, is like a baseball player coming up to bat: he carries three bats to the plate, swinging them. Finally, he drops all but one, facing the pitcher with a bat that now feels light. The subject here has recently unburdened himself of a physical or emotional problem, or both, and he is celebrating, if only in his subconscious mind. All this is fine—if taken for what it is, recognized as a psychological device enabling the subject to better face life, just as the batter now is able to face the pitcher, that bat powerful in his grip, yet the feeling one of lightness, flexibility.

THIS IS NOT THE TIME FOR THE SUBJECT TO BECOME TIED DOWN, EITHER IN BUSINESS DEALS OR IN HIS PERSONAL LIFE.

Wait and see. Be cheerful.

Be enthusiastic without being wasteful.

The Truth usually shines through here. That's why the subject has dialed to numbers that total 3, giving the Jupiter-Sagittarius ninth-house symbol. Through use of intuition, or "higher mind," the subject has caught a three-dimensional glimpse of his own world, his life, the people surrounding him.

As an indicator of subconscious thought, this total tells the subject to look around, to gain, to avoid being anchored down, for social activities are going to be stepped up and contacts are going to be made—and Lady Luck is putting in an appearance.

IF THE TOTAL IS FOUR:

Number 4 is the square, a fact recognized by both mathematicians and numerologists. It is of the Earth element. It is associated with Uranus, but also contains elements of the Sun. Thus, 4 is related, to a large extent, to the zodiacal signs of Aquarius and Leo. It is symbolized by restriction, attention to details, plain, old-fashioned hard work.

The subject, whose total is 4, is tempted to pass on the details to others, to skip a step, to move ahead. Uranus pushes for a change, while the Sun tempts toward immediate glory and publicity. BUT THE SUBCONSCIOUS, THROUGH THE THOUGHT DIAL TOTAL, WARNS THAT THE DETAILS CANNOT BE TRUSTED TO OTHERS. Otherwise the subject will have to retrace his steps, to move back. This is a time of testing and discipline. Determination must be a keynote for the subject. The subconscious, here, is laying stress upon strength, determination, the details, the plans necessary for change and creative action. BUT THAT CHANGE, THAT ACTION, IS FOR THE FUTURE. PERHAPS THE NEAR FUTURE. BUT IT IS NOT FOR NOW!

Number 4 is solid. And as mathematician Constance Reid states, it is one of the first and most permanent ideas in number—that 4 is the earth number. It is a square similar to the "square," or 90-degree aspect, in astrology. It is a test of strength. And if the subject recognizes it as such, he can be patient, knowing that quiet planning now, a gathering of strength, a look around at his assets, can be instrumental to success, perhaps even spectacular success in the future. Careless action now, weakness, will surely lead to disappointment, to failure, to loss.

With the 4 total, the subject had better not listen to the advice of friends . . . *at this moment*. The tendency is for friends, no matter how well-meaning, to give advice that would be good in the near-future. BUT NOT FOR NOW! Hopes, wishes, aspirations, creative urges, all of these combine to form GIGANTIC TEMPTATION. The subject wants to break away, to be free from confinement (the square)—but, says the Thought Dial (subconscious), he must first make absolutely sure his foundation is SOLID.

Attention to duty is a necessity. Knowledge of limitations is another. This is the time to BUILD for the FUTURE. To build, not to stand atop an incomplete foundation and shout from the rooftop; again, this is a time of TESTING.

Here is another fact, perhaps the most important of all, in considering 4 as a Thought Dial subconscious-thought indicator:

BE AWARE OF OTHER THAN MATERIAL VALUES! Be aware of spiritual and moral issues. In plainer, perhaps less metaphysical language, check your relations with the public (public relations), be sure there is imagination and fire, not just earth and concrete, to your plans, projects, dreams, dealings.

Be patient. Check and double-check.

Your day is coming! It's not today, however.

IF THE TOTAL IS FIVE:

Number 5 is associated with the planet Mercury, and with the zodiacal signs of Gemini and Virgo: it is a symbol of investigation, of analysis, of creativity, relations with members of the opposite sex—it is a number and symbol of romance, of probing, of investigation, curiosity and life itself. The subject, dialing this total, is being told (through subconscious symbolism), to take the road leading to CHANGE, TRAVEL, VARIETY.

Number 5 is the digit, the symbol of COMMUNICATION. Now there is freedom, just as with number 4 there was restriction. The subject, with this total as a subconscious-thought indicator, is thinking of change and travel—and this total ENCOURAGES SUCH A COURSE OF ACTION. The important thing is action. This is the time for change, for revision, for creative, progressive thinking. The element here is Air.

Ambition is keynoted—there is no standing still. Movement and rhythm are emphasized. This is the time for a publicity campaign, for writing, communicating, putting across ideas.

Excesses, of course, must be avoided. This total, as a subconscious-thought indicator, tends to encourage lust, the giving in to base appetites. A balance must be struck. Otherwise a romance (for example) can turn into a sordid affair.

It is here, however, that impulsive action is to be encouraged. The subject, dialing this total, should trust first impressions, should be encouraged to make the try, no matter how high the goal. INTEREST IN MEMBERS OR A MEMBER OF THE OPPOSITE SEX IS VERY MUCH IN THE PICTURE. Natural attraction is revealed—the overall pattern is good, encouraging.

This is the time for the subject to prove, to INVESTIGATE. New paths are suggested. Certainly, a change is recommended. It is likely that the subject is concerned with romance, the possibility of marriage, or children—or all of these. The answers to speculation concerning these matters is positive, in the affirmative. Emphasis is placed upon greater FREEDOM of thought and action. This is obtained, the subconscious states, through INVESTIGATION and EXPERIMENTATION.

Recreation, vacation—the subject should attempt to *work through play*.

Creative projects should NOT be neglected.

Now is the time to speculate, to take a chance, to seek SELF-EXPRESSION and personal advancement.

Personal magnetism and attractiveness are on the side of the subject at this time.

Write, communicate thoughts, dramatize, travel, open your heart, these are part of the overall pattern, as indicated by the Thought Dial.

This is NOT the time to be confined, to stick to outmoded or "proven" methods.

Number 5, as a total, LOOKS TO THE FUTURE through creativity.

Best advice: NOW IS THE TIME—do it!

IF THE TOTAL IS SIX:

Number 6 is similar, in some ways, to the digit 2. Number 6 is the diplomat, is associated with the planet Venus, has much to do with domesticity, conditions in the home, relations with relatives.

OFTEN, WHEN A SUBJECT DIALS A TOTAL OF 6, HE IS THINKING OF A CHANGE IN THE HOME. This change could be emotional or physical—a change of residence, for instance.

It is necessary, with this total, for the subject to investigate family conditions, matters in his own home. It does no good to conquer the world only to fail at home. Financial matters, marriage, contracts, public and home relations—all symbolized by this number.

The subject, through his subconscious, is being advised to be sympathetic. This is NOT the time to force issues, to be "tough." It is the time for handling persons and problems diplomatically. Others depend on the subject for a sympathetic ear, a shoulder to cry on. SOMEONE CLOSE TO THE SUBJECT MAY FLOUT THE LAWS OF CONVENTION. The subject, instead of being shocked or preaching, should be DIPLOMATIC and SYMPATHETIC.

The elements are a *combination* of Earth and Air. And that tells a story: the subject, by dialing this total, knows that he must *combine* practicality with visionary foresight.

That is the answer to all of his current problems: A COMBINATION OF EARTHINESS AND AIRY VISION.

Responsibility is a keynote. The weight of many problems—in connection with home, loved ones, family—rests on the subject's shoulders. HE SHOULD BE MADE TO SEE THAT THESE PROBLEMS WILL ALMOST SOLVE THEMSELVES. He should not complicate them through forceful action. HE SHOULD LISTEN AND WAIT.

The subconscious mind, through the symbolism of the Thought Dial, tells the subject to take a stand for impartiality, for justice, for rational thinking. Otherwise, there are bound to be complications.

Number 6, quite often, is associated with the throat or voice. It is through *measured thought and speech* that the subject gains and is able to aid loved ones. Harmony is the desire here. To gain this harmony requires skill, diplomacy—and a sincere desire to see justice done.

THIS IS THE TIME (says the subconscious) TO SERIOUSLY CONSIDER MATTERS OF THE HOME . . . AS WELL AS MARRIAGE.

There is responsibility here. Just as with 5 there was romance . . . with 6 there is the responsibility of the home, of marriage, of the *results* of romance.

The subject is advised to be GENEROUS, both in willingness to negotiate disputes, to forgive errors, and to help those in financial need. There is a tendency here, as with the number 2, to collect, to be possessive. The subject must be on his guard, lest he fight for POSSESSIONS, for books he will never read, for dishes he will never use, and so on. COMMON SENSE—a sense of justice, maturity—these are the qualities that now count, that are very essential.

The subconscious, with this total, is urging restraint, pointing up the need to attend to matters at home, and is pushing forth for justice, compassion and diplomacy.

WAIT! BE PATIENT! AND REMEMBER THAT RIGHT NOW THE WORLD FOR YOU IS YOUR HOME!

IF THE TOTAL IS SEVEN:

Number 7 is associated with the planet Neptune: it is very similar in influence in that the subject here is apt to be a victim of self-deception. It is not that others are trying to fool him, but he has a tendency to see persons and situations the way he wishes they could be, instead of the way they actually exist.

Number 7, as a total on the Thought Dial here, points to a basic loneliness. The subject is independent, sensitive, filled with pride. It is a matter of righting the world in his own mind, of convincing himself—when, all the time, it is ONLY IN HIS MIND.

No contracts here. No signing of legal documents. This is a time to wait and see. The subconscious, through the Thought Dial total, is trying to say that the aspects of the subject's life are now NEPTUNIAN, which means there is a lack of solidity. This is a time for FAITH. But there is a fine line between faith, and willingness to FALL FOR A LINE. That's putting it roughly, perhaps, but it is the truth—and nothing can lead to disappointment and failure faster than contracts now, belief in those who offer only a sincere "front."

There is association here with hospitals, institutions: there is apt to be a feeling of confinement. The tendency is to veer toward the romantic, to express willingness to go along with fantastic schemes. Thus the obvious answer is to WAIT, especially in connection with partnerships, businesswise or in relation to marriage.

THIS IS THE TIME TO ANALYZE, TO PERFECT, TO EXAMINE, TO SCRUTINIZE PERSONS AND SITUATIONS. Take nothing for granted!

This is a time for critical SELF-EXAMINATION. This is the time for the subject to be ALONE. No one else can solve his problems. The solution comes from his INNER-SELF. Number 7, as a total, is not easy to comprehend, because it represents a PERIOD OF TIME, or a thought, that is far from "easy." It is difficult, just as religion, or inspiration, or intuition, is difficult to pin down or to evaluate on a material basis.

There is a desire for PERFECTION here, which can lead to brooding and worry. On the positive side, however, the subject can aim high—can do his best and achieve much—if he realizes that perfection is not a necessity.

THE LESSON TO LEARN HERE IS TO BE ALONE WITHOUT SUFFERING THE PANGS OF LONELINESS.

The subject must be prepared to REJECT false flattery. He must be discriminating. For if he fails to SEEK the best, he will be unhappy.

As a subconscious total, number 7 (Water element) points up the necessity of eliminating persons and things NOT ESSENTIAL. The subject is being told to TRIM DOWN.

To get rid of waste. To accept solitude as something POSITIVE, not negative. This is a SPIRITUAL number and symbol: it is a sure sign that the subject must re-evaluate his needs, desires, likes and dislikes. THE SUBJECT MUST GET TO KNOW HIMSELF. His outlook changes. His perspective improves.

IT IS ADVISABLE FOR HIM TO GET CLOSE TO NATURE AND ESPECIALLY TO HIS OWN NATURE.

No contacts here. Face reality. Avoid self-deception. Get off by yourself. Analyze—seek truth, perfection.

AND STOP BROODING!

IF THE TOTAL IS EIGHT:

This is the power number, associated with Saturn and pressure, responsibility—material gain is here, but along with it, plenty of hard work.

The element is Earth; the subject who dials this total as a subconscious indicator is concerned with finances, added responsibility, outside pressures perhaps involving marriage, members of the opposite sex and problems connected with business investments.

The subconscious, here, is saying, PUSH AHEAD, NOW IS THE TIME TO STRIKE! The Thought Dial (symbolizing the subconscious) urges action here, willingness to invest, to accept added pressures and responsibility—and that responsibility could be a new business, an investment, or marriage, or creative activity, including willingness to have a child.

Number 8, perhaps, is one of the most powerful of the number symbols; it is sex, the creative urge, the giving of one's self.

THERE IS NOTHING HALFWAY HERE. IT IS ALL THE WAY OR NOTHING AT ALL. If the subject is wondering about putting a finger or a toe in—the Thought Dial tells him it is all the way, a complete dive into the water—or forget the project altogether.

Career, standing in the community, attainment of desires, a push up the ladder—all these things, and others, are symbolized by this total.

Lead without being the bully. Exercise authority without resorting to dictatorial methods. This is the executive number; the subject has asked for certain authority and has worked for it—now he has it and this is NO TIME TO SHIRK RESPONSIBILITY.

Number 8 is 4 doubled, intensified. The details, it is

assumed, have been taken care of, basic lessons learned.
NOW IS THE TIME TO APPLY THESE LESSONS, THAT KNOWL-
EDGE.

Avoid pettiness. Think and act big! That is the only way
here, according to the message screamed by the subconscious.

The subject must be THE ORGANIZER. He must be
prepared to grasp the most complicated situation at a
glance. He should be urged to act upon his intuition, his
judgment, his overall knowledge. THIS IS NOT THE TIME TO
BE SWAYED OR INFLUENCED BY SMALLER PERSONS.

Number 8 is money, finances, investments, building,
commercial success, the marketing of material. The subject here, must assume and *live* the role of EXECUTIVE.

The Earth and Saturn elements of the symbol, plus the
tenth-house associations, show that the subject, to succeed,
must push, must exercise power, must invest, advertise,
work and organize.

Don't wait too long! And this applies to BOTH personal
and business activities. MARRIAGE, BUSINESS. Those two
sum up the keys to this symbol.

THIS IS THE TIME TO MAKE YOUR OWN OPPORTUNITIES—
that is the message of the Thought Dial.

The subject is not likely to succeed in a project that HAS
ALREADY BEEN STARTED.

On the other hand, he DOES succeed in ORGANIZING a
project himself, in taking a hank and a hair and some
bones and putting together something that begins to PULSE
WITH LIFE.

The symbol is clear enough. It is up to the subject to
take note of the implications here. His subconscious tells
him he is ready. NOW IS THE TIME FOR HIM TO BE
CONVINCED THAT INDEED HE IS READY!

Remember, don't wait too long!

IF THE TOTAL IS NINE:

The subconscious, here, is making it plain that a situation, a relationship, a phase, a cycle of life, is COMPLETED.
This is NOT the time to hang on. This IS the time to finish
projects, to get rid of burdens that are not rightly the
subject's responsibility in the first place.

Here, the subject—through his subconscious—is being
told to seek new paths, new persons, new loves. The old is
over. He must recognize this fact, no matter how difficult
that task may be.

Number 9 is associated with the planet Mars, is of the Fire element, is related to personality, to independence in the spirit of breaking away from restrictions represented by the past.

If the subject is concerned about whether to begin a project, the answer is simple: DON'T!

If the subject is worried about whether to end a relationship, business or personal, the answer is equally simple: DO!

This, perhaps, is one of the clearest symbols. THE SUBCONSCIOUS RELATES THE THEME OF PUBLIC RELATIONS on a UNIVERSAL SCALE. This IS the time to advertise, to let others know the value of products the subject has to offer.

Number 9 is the symbol of UNIVERSAL APPEAL. It is also, on the positive side, the number of selfless love. It is the number of the humanitarian, the nurse, doctor, teacher.

But, on the negative side, it tells a story of burden. Perhaps the subject is being taken advantage of by another: he is carrying someone else's financial load, pulling more, much more than his fair share. And this "pulling" can apply both to professional and personal matters. NOW IS THE TIME TO TAKE STOCK, TO MAKE A BREAK FOR NEW DIRECTIONS, FOR GREATER FREEDOM, PEACE OF MIND.

Simply put, the subconscious is strongly aware of a situation that no longer is tolerable. Perhaps the "situation" is represented by false hope, a false friend, a false promise. Or, perhaps the friend, the promise the hope, is sincere—but it will not work, not at this time. TO HANG ON WOULD BE TO IMPRISON ONE'S SELF.

This total on the Thought Dial, as a subconscious indicator, urges compassion—but a compassionate attitude based upon *practicality*. Now is the time for OTHERS TO HELP THEMSELVES. They can do this only if the subject REMOVES HIMSELF AS A CRUTCH.

Determination is required. It is certainly not easy to make a break, to take a new direction, a different course of action. Yet, it must be done! And it is to be done for the good of others, as well as for the subject's welfare.

In business matters, a relationship breaks up, but it is not a pretty sight, because the break-up is not based on a mutual desire. Usually, it is the subject who must take the initiative.

THIS IS THE TIME—with this Thought Dial total—TO

TRAVEL FAR AND WIDE . . . to seek new knowledge, to gain and adhere to a philosophy of life, one with enough fiber so that it does not tear at the slightest pull.

This is a summing up, the end of a cycle, preparation for the new.

FINISH. COMPLETE. SUMMARIZE. FINALIZE. These are key words.

A long journey might well be in order here. Certainly, "journeys of the mind" are indicated.

DO NOT BROOD ABOUT THE PAST, LEARN FROM PAST EXPERIENCES AND APPLY THOSE LESSONS TO THE FUTURE.

And stop spoiling one you think you love!

IF THE TOTAL IS ELEVEN:

This is one of the two double numbers recognized in this system. Numbers 11 and 22 are not reduced to single digits. All others are. And so this number, 11, is one of the most unusual of all: it represents a higher version of 2, it is the Moon and Uranus, it is intuition and, most of all, it is the TEACHER. The subject, dialing this total on the Thought Dial, is concerned with UNSEEN FORCES. He is able to sense that something of importance is about to occur, but he can't quite put his finger on it.

As in number 2, diplomacy is called for. No forcing of issues. The element here is Air—motives must be of the highest order.

OTHERS WILL LOOK TO THE SUBJECT, then expect him to teach and, if necessary, to preach the law. Number 11 is similar to 7 in that religion in the highest sense of the word is involved. IF THE QUESTION IS WHETHER TO BY-PASS THE LAW, OR TO CLOSE ONE'S EYES TO SOMEONE WHO IS SKIRTING THE LAW, the answer is . . . DO NOT BECOME INVOLVED! Or, in plainer words, PLAY IT STRAIGHT!

If the subject is tempted to be weak here, he is warned (by the subconscious message) that he may get involved to a deeper extent than he dreamed possible. Hands off anything that isn't really honest to the letter. This applies to business and personal dealings—and to the subject's dealing with himself. CONSCIENCE is the keyword here. Pay attention to it!

The intuition is highlighted. THE SUBJECT, at this time, IS STRONGLY ADVISED TO TRUST HIS INTUITION. This is the time to hesitate, to listen to the INNER VOICE, to be cautious, to examine (and closely!) the motives of those who may be posing (or hiding) under the cloak of religion or charity, or otherwise. ASK THAT THE CARDS BE PLACED FACE UP ON THE TABLE!

This is the time, says the Thought Dial, to be IDEALISTIC.

This is the time to probe the unknown: interest indicated in astrology, electricity, television, aviation, outer space, the occult, extrasensory perception, psychology, numerology, hand analysis, studies that lead to SELF-REVELATION.

YOU LEARN HERE BY TEACHING! Accept requests to be a GROUP LEADER. You advance by DOING.

The subject, dialing this total as a subconscious thought symbol, is concerned with a QUESTION OF FAITH. Faith in an individual, an idea, a government, a political party, a business enterprise—FAITH IN HIMSELF. In answer to this dilemma: LISTEN TO THE INNER VOICE WHETHER YOU WISH TO CALL IT INTUITION OR CONSCIENCE, or whatever.

It is necessary for the subject to take time to KNOW HIMSELF. He must clear his mind of "clutterings" and get at his true source of inspiration.

The subject must go after SELF-RECOGNITION. He must first know himself before he can teach or help others. Otherwise, there will be unhappiness, self-annoyance, dissension.

In all, this is a powerful symbol: it is related to friends, hopes, wishes, children, relations with members of the opposite sex.

It is here, under this influence, that the subject asks himself concerning his lover: IS SHE MY FRIEND, TOO?

Much of the future depends upon the answer!

Don't rush into anything. When the tendency is to wait, to hesitate—do so.

IF THE TOTAL IS TWENTY-TWO:

This double number, like 11, is retained instead of being reduced to a single digit, as are other totals—it is a master symbol in that it is the CREATIVE BUILDER. Number 22 appears to be related to the planet Pluto. The element here is Water. As a subconscious indicator on the Thought Dial, it tells of the necessity of thinking of projects as a WHOLE. The details, in this case, must be left to others: the subject cannot afford to be bogged down with matters of minor importance. The message here is simple: HAVE VISION, EXERCISE INTUITIVE INTELLECT—don't try to do everything yourself!

Number 22 is the master architect: it is a number of

BUILDING. But the subject should realize that his subconscious is also telling him not to be afraid to TEAR DOWN.

Tear down and REBUILD, if necessary. This is no time to stick with a losing proposition—UNLESS YOU ARE PREPARED TO MAKE IMPROVEMENTS AND STREAMLINE THE OPERATION.

The subject, in dialing a total of 22, is expressing *subconscious knowledge* of this fact. He is capable of succeeding once this knowledge is MADE KNOWN TO HIS CONSCIOUS MIND, as it is being done here.

THIS IS THE TIME TO CARRY OUT IDEALS. This is the time, shouts the subconscious, to turn dreams into realities. Now is the time, without further delay, to put PLANS ON PAPER. Now, with all due speed, is the time to realize that inspiration is of solid substance and can be applied toward ultimate SUCCESS.

Number 22 is a symbol of success. That's why routine, details, must be left to others. The subject, dialing this total, must be the DREAMER OF PRACTICAL DREAMS. And that means he must MAKE his dreams COME TRUE .

This is *not* the time for false claims or false pride. This *is* the time to PRODUCE. Money will be forthcoming, perhaps from business or marital partners, from those who are inspired by the subject's FAITH and BELIEF.

In this way it can be seen that INTANGIBLES help make the subject's dreams and visions turn to REALITIES.

The subject is being told here that pettiness, inefficiency—both in his business and personal life—must be eliminated. The total of 22, as a subconscious symbol, warns that movements, campaigns, plans, ideas, hopes, wishes, must be on a GRAND SCALE. Anything small here seems doomed to failure. Even if the project is not a large one in a physical sense, it should be in an IDEALISTIC one.

Number 22 is a higher version of 4. This presumes that the DETAILS are being well attended to, that associates can be trusted—that the subject has authority to BUILD UP, or TEAR DOWN, for the purpose of reorganizing. Otherwise, the subject should work to make these presumptions ACTUALITIES.

Diplomacy is necessary here. Intuition and sensitivity are also requisites. Ambition is keynoted. Where number 8 is concentrated, to a large extent, on FINANCIAL GAIN . . . 22 longs for RECOGNITION. There is much to live up to here.

If the subject has been trying to SKIMP ON IDEALS ... then he is not happy at this moment.

There is power here: the goal is the highest, but it can be reached. AND NO COMPROMISE SHOULD BE MADE!

That, perhaps, is the key to this symbol: The subject is being told that the time for compromise is *past*.

Move upward and onward. And if there is something or someone blocking the way, build around, or over, or under—but build!

8

The How and Why of Thought Dial

In the previous section, detailed indications of what the subconscious tries to convey, through Thought Dial symbolism, were presented. Questions, of course, probably will continue to arise as to how and why the Thought Dial can be utilized as an instrument to impart this knowledge.

All of the answers are *not known*. But some of them are. As stated, the Thought Dial is based on the theory that memory *continues*, a sort of reflex action: memory is always *there*, even if the subject is not conscious of it.

Perhaps a good analogy would be a line, a time line. The beginning of the line is the *past*. The line continues to the *present*, and on to the *future*. The line has a beginning (the past), a middle (the present) and an end (the future). Memory is like that line. It is there, from beginning to end, perhaps to infinity, as suggested by J. B. Rhine whose experiments appear to verify Dr. Stromberg's belief that memory survives bodily death.

Memory is thus familiar with basic *number symbols*, the oldest symbols known to man, followed by symbols of an astrological nature.

In his syndicated newspaper feature, "Mirror of Your Mind," Joseph Whitney asked, "Can memory be unconscious?" His answer is an unequivocal *yes*. He declares that unconscious memories influence many of our general behavior patterns. And he concludes by stating that "Conscious memory influences behavior by direct recall, but unconscious memory does so without our awareness."

The unconscious memory, it can be presumed, is familiar with number symbols, seeking them out via the Thought Dial.

Now it may be asked, "Who said numbers had any special meanings, anyhow?"

The answer to that can be found by consulting mathematicians who have made a serious study of numbers. Mr. Tobey, in his introduction, also goes into the story of numbers, their properties, meanings and personalities. Numerologists, too, although they are often frowned upon by academicians, have kept records for thousands of years, records based on research and experiments. The numbers have come to be associated with certain meanings, and the numbers stand as symbols, each telling a story with which *the subconscious is presumed to be familiar.*

Dr. Carl Jung has repeatedly asserted this to be true—that *planets and numbers* represent valuable keys to the unlocking of the subconscious.

It was the late Dr. Ernest Jones, biographer of Freud, who pointed out his subject's interest in the special meanings of numbers. He does so in his *The Life and Work of Sigmund Freud.** In that distinguished work, Dr. Jones reveals Freud's fascination with parapsychology, including psychoanalysis and telepathy, and dreams and telepathy. Freud's greatest student, of course, was Jung, who constantly pleaded the case for astrology. Freud himself ascribed special powers to numbers and declared that the figures 28 and 23 were important in his own life.

These are some of the answers—or at least *hints* of what the answers *might* be—in the "why and how" of the Thought Dial.

Just as it is possible to cultivate the "mind's eye" (create mental images, develop a strong mental visual sense), so it is also possible to cultivate the subconscious and its familiarity with well-known symbols (numbers and planets).

In his article "You Can Cultivate the Mind's Eye," Bruce Bliven points out that capable mathematicians usually have a strong visual sense. Bliven, in his study, says

* Basic Books, Inc., New York.

mathematicians are able to picture complicated problems. He presents, as an example, mathematician John von Neumann, who apparently could "see" the final result of a long problem—see it written in his mind.

Perhaps the subconscious *is* the "mind's eye." It enables us to "see" when we give it the opportunity of expressing itself through numbers (Thought Dial).

9

Direct Questions Answered

In the section on subconscious thoughts, general indications were given for the various Thought Dial totals. In many instances, these *general* analyses *will* provide not only the answer to specific problems, but also cover numerous other current aspects of the subject's life.

However, to be more specific, the Thought Dial can be applied to the answering of *special* problems. At times, the answers will coincide with the subconscious indicator. That is, a total of 9, dialed with a *specific* problem in mind, will be similar to the 9 total as a subconscious indicator. This is as it should be.

It is interesting to note that many times, when the subject thinks of a direct or specific question, he also reveals the *birth date* of a person the question is concerned with. Other times, through the Thought Dial, he gives his *own* zodiacal sign.

For example, the subject thinks of a specific question. At all times, the question should be formed clearly and as briefly as possible. Then, after the subject concentrates, he is to dial three numbers. The operator then totals and reduces to a single number, unless the total happens to be 11 or 22.

Suppose the total is 2. Number 2 is associated with the Moon, which rules Cancer. The subject himself, or one important to his question or problem, can be presumed (many times) to be born under Cancer, between June 22 and July 23, OR UNDER THE OPPOSITE SIGN: CAPRICORN (from December 22 to January 20).

In other words, the total on the Thought Dial reveals a significant birth date in relation to the subject's problem or question. The birth dates revealed are as follows:

IF THE TOTAL IS 1: Leo or Aquarius—From July 24 to August 23 or from January 1 to February 19.

IF THE TOTAL IS 2: Cancer or Capricorn—From June 22 to July 23, or from December 22 to January 20.

IF THE TOTAL IS 3: Sagittarius or Gemini—From November 23 to December 21, or from May 22 to June 21.

IF THE TOTAL IS 4: Aquarius or Leo—From January 21 to February 19, or from July 24 to August 23.

IF THE TOTAL IS 5: Gemini or Sagittarius—From May 22 to June 21, or from November 23 to December 21; or Virgo or Pisces (August 24 to September 23—February 20 to March 20).

IF THE TOTAL IS 6: Taurus or Scorpio—From April 21 to May 21, or from October 24 to November 22; or Libra or Aries (September 24 to October 23—March 21 to April 20).

IF THE TOTAL IS 7: Pisces or Virgo—From February 20 to March 20, or from August 24 to September 23.

IF THE TOTAL IS 8: Capricorn or Cancer—From December 22 to January 20, or from June 22 to July 23.

IF THE TOTAL IS 9: Aries or Libra—From March 21 to April 20, or from September 24 to October 23.

IF THE TOTAL IS 11: Aquarius or Leo—From January 21 to February 19, or from July 24 to August 23, or Cancer or Capricorn—from June 22 to July 23, or December 22 to January 20.

IF THE TOTAL IS 22: Scorpio or Taurus—From October 24 to November 22, or from April 21 to May 2.

Now, not in all cases will the birth date revealed appear significant. In many cases, however, it is either the subject's own zodiacal sign, or belongs to a person currently significant in the question, or one *who will be in the future*.

With practice in delineation, the operator of the Thought Dial will develop skill, just as in the case of interpreting a horoscope.

These interpretations, which follow, provide a cornerstone, a starting point, a basis—a basis evolved after some twenty years of experiment and research.

I have found that these basic interpretations work. Clients or subjects are aided. The operator, using this system, often finds a key and looks for certain things in the horoscope, or personality makeup, of the subject. The Thought Dial leads the way. From there on, it is necessary for the operator to develop skill. And it is up to the subject to analyze and derive what benefits he can from Thought Dial indications.

Remember, the subject must concentrate on a SPECIFIC question. He must form it clearly, concisely in his own mind. When he has done this, he is to dial three numbers on the Thought Dial. The operator then totals the digits, reducing the answer to a single number between 1 and 9, with the exceptions of 11 or 22, which are the only double numbers not reduced. The subject THINKS and DIALS; he does not reveal his question.

IF THE TOTAL IS 1:

Specifically, the subject's question concerns a new project, or a new association, either business or personal. In many cases, the subject has met someone and is romantically inclined toward that person. The subconscious, through the Thought Dial, encourages the subject to pursue NEW PERSONS, PROJECTS, and paths that lead to greater independence of thought and action through a BREAK WITH THE PAST.

Significant zodiacal signs, in connection with this question, are apt to be LEO or AQUARIUS.

The question itself is one that evolves around initiative, creative ability, new starts, original thinking, and could be associated with affairs of the heart. Children, too, might well be involved.

The closest to a direct answer would be: GO YOUR OWN WAY ON THIS MATTER. It is not a time to follow others, Rather, the Thought Dial indicates that only through direct, original, perhaps daring, action can you succeed.

The question, most likely, is one that involves pioneering action. And the subject is apt to be concerned with a BREAK FROM TRADITION.

The answer, provided by the subconscious (via the Thought Dial), is that a break is necessary for a positive conclusion to this problem.

The subject wants to know whether to go back, or to move ahead. The answer is to MOVE AHEAD.

Children, entertainment, creative ways of entertaining, are also suggested. New ways to advertise. New ways to serve in the entertainment fields—all these are favored in answer to the question being asked.

The subject should, in dialing this total, be encouraged to emerge as an INDIVIDUAL who LEADS the way.

A direct answer would be, YES—go ahead! Be confident that original, forceful methods will work in this case. No turning back, not now!

IF THE TOTAL IS 2:

The subject himself was born under Cancer or Capricorn, or someone important in this question might have been born under one of those zodiacal signs. The question itself is one that covers the areas of SECURITY, HOME, ONE OF THE PARENTS. In dialing this total, the subject shows he is much aware of a need for security, a bank account, the collecting of data, which will enable him to prove his worth.

One part of the answer to this question is: STOP BROODING! Worry here can only hinder, not help. And the subject, as his subconscious reveals, has been doing a lot of worrying, much of it needless.

In answer to the question: The subject must collect data, facts, and he must also be prepared to accept a budget. There will be limitations to what he can do. BUT HE CAN BEST SUCCEED BY GOING ALONG WITH THE TIDE, by *quiet acceptance*. There is no better time to be a diplomat than in connection with this problem!

Someone in his own home can help the subject. And, in answer to the question, the *answer is not to try to answer at this time*. Wait. Be patient. Let the storm blow over. Hold the line. Prepare a presentation of the facts and, when called upon, present them with diplomacy and modesty.

In other words, the time for decision has NOT YET ARRIVED. This is the time for watchful waiting—but NOT for brooding.

A woman, especially an older woman, appears to figure prominently in the outcome of this problem.

The subconscious stresses the need for careful consideration of the future. This can be done, first, by working out a budget and sticking to it.

IF THE TOTAL IS 3:

CONFUSION is the keynote here. In answer to the subject's question, nothing can be accomplished until he settles down. It does no good to try probing in all directions at once. Wasted energy indicated here, in a question related to long journeys and ideas of an expansive nature, and to social activities. Public relations, advertising—and persons (perhaps the subject himself) born under the zodiacal signs of Sagittarius or Gemini—may all be involved in the answer to this query.

The outcome appears favorable, whatever the question, because the subconscious cries only for STEADINESS, a veering AWAY from confusion—and does NOT cry in anything resembling panic.

The subject, dialing this total, does not appear to know JUST WHAT IT IS he wants. Curiosity runs high. And the question, very likely, has to do with the possibility of FINDING OUT MORE—possibly the *theme* of the query has to do with social activities, and most certainly it concerns one who is far away, or is planning to move away.

A sense of humor is a necessity if the subject is to arrive at a constructive solution. Otherwise, he is apt to create trouble where none existed.

OFTEN A SUBJECT WHO IS MERELY TESTING THE DIAL— one who has a predetermined attitude that there is "nothing to it"—will dial a 3 total. This is the subconscious symbol of little or no concentration. The answer to the question—if one is actually being asked—also lies in this sphere: a call for greater concentration, attention to details, an attitude based on facts not fancy.

The problem or question here is NOT as serious as the subject might believe. And circumstances may well take it out of his hands before he can do anything about it.

IF THE TOTAL IS 4:

The answer to this question is more work; the subject cannot escape from the routine, which he is coming to abhor. Now is not the time.

Either the subject himself, or one closely related to the problem, was born under Aquarius, or perhaps under the sign of Leo. Hoping and wishing will not make it so. Passing the buck won't, either. There are details, many of them considered unpleasant, which have to be attended to before anything else can be accomplished.

Specifically, the question concerns a "blocking in," restriction, a lack of freedom—the lack caused either by a person or situation, or both.

The answer, based on the 4 symbol, lies with the subject: he must make up his mind to finish what was started.

No, don't trust details to others.

Yes, do prepare to work hard and harder—there is a square, a block that stands in the way, an obstacle: this is a test, and to be a test of any value it must *test* you. Knowing this, the subject should be prepared to WORK and WAIT.

No, do not make sudden changes.

Yes, do plan for a change in the FUTURE.

You are not imprisoned. You make your own prison by feeling that all avenues to escape are sealed.

The answer, in general, is negative—BUT ONLY FOR THE TIME BEING!

The subject is concerned with LACK: lack of finances, lack of love, lack of freedom, lack of appreciation, and the list could be extended. BUT THE ANSWER LIES IN PATIENCE, GRIT, DETERMINATION, WILLINGNESS TO DO THE RIGHT THING AND SEE THE PROJECT THROUGH TO ITS COMPLETION.

The solution here could come through a younger person, perhaps one of the subject's own children. A loved one aids here—and the subject is grateful he waited.

The answer is WAIT.

And no excuses!

IF THE TOTAL IS 5:

The subject, thinking of a specific question and dialing this total, is apt to have sex on his mind!

That is, the subject is concerned with a member of the opposite sex: the subconscious, via this symbol, reveals that love, creative thinking, etc., is necessary to the solution of the problem.

The answer is generally affirmative. Marriage is strongly indicated. So is change, travel, communication of thoughts through writing or some other art.

Yes, now is the time to expand and experiment.

No, now is *not* the time to practice enforced economy. The BUDGET must be STRETCHED!

The zodiacal signs involved here are Gemini and Sagittarius, and Virgo and Pisces.

Love and marriage are highlighted. But the subject, if he is specifically asking about marriage, should make sure

there is MORE THAN JUST PHYSICAL ATTRACTION IN-
VOLVED. Otherwise, he will find that the honeymoon is soon
over.

The subconscious, through this symbol, seems to be
telling of the necessity to COMMUNICATE, to travel, even
though the journeys be short ones, to keep in touch with
friends, relatives, those who have—in the recent past—
been neglected by the subject.

Yes, express yourself by writing, by INVESTING IN YOUR
OWN TALENTS.

NO, do not listen to those who are urging you to wait,
to pull a surprise in the future. NOW IS THE TIME, not
later.

The answer to the question, put simply, is: MAKE A
CHANGE, even if travel is involved. AND DON'T RUN AWAY
FROM ROMANCE. You will only have to return!

In conclusion, calm down! The number 5 symbol is
indicative that the subject is "keyed up."

Self-expression is the best way of getting rid of this
tension.

IF THE TOTAL IS 6:

Persons dialing this total are very often concerned with
a domestic situation. THE DIRECT ANSWER TO THE QUES-
TION IS: A change in the home, through adjustment or
readjustment, is very necessary. Putting off the situation
will not help. It will, instead, aggravate the problem.

Too, there is apt to be concern with the *voice* in some
manner or other.

Basically, it is a matter of rediscovering loved ones. Of
adjusting to their needs. Of clearing up a situation in the
home that has been allowed to hang on and on.

Yes, DO move, if that seems to be the only solution.
Yes, a change of residence is apt to prove beneficial.

Straighten out family differences. The answer to the
question is generally NEGATIVE—but only until those matters involving family and home are attended to, then the
situation brightens.

Birth dates (zodiacal signs) involved in this question
appear to be: Taurus and Scorpio—Libra and Aries.

Money matters could be involved here because a move,
a "brightening" of the atmosphere through decorations,
fixtures, new furniture, appear necessary.

DRAMA AND VOICE—artistic expression—these, too,
come through as a result of this subconscious symbol.

Perhaps a member of the subject's family, or the subject himself, is concerned with these matters.

There are some loose ends that need tying. The subject, if he seeks a solution by further delay, is in for a rude shock. NOW IS THE TIME TO STRAIGHTEN OUT MATTERS IN THE HOME. Now, not later.

A plea that "these things cost money" is a poor excuse.

The answer to this question lies in direct action to remedy an oversight that should have been remedied long ago.

IF THE TOTAL IS 7:

This, it appears, is a case of self-deception. It isn't that others are attempting to fool the subject or to mislead him: but, in connection with this question, he seems intent on fooling *himself*.

Zodiacal signs involved here are Pisces and Virgo.

A relationship appears to be breaking up: a contract is not valid. The answer to the question, briefly stated—is YES *and* NO.

No, your ideas about a person or situation will not hold water. In the near future your illusions will be shattered.

Yes, you will recover and go on to fulfill your mission, your hopes and your wishes.

You will do this by ridding yourself of false concepts. You will be in a better position to face reality once a Neptunian situation is eliminated.

You will gain *inner strength* through present trials. There is a feeling of restriction here. The subject is apt to find himself confined due to a minor illness: his freedom of movement is hampered, sometimes because of a foot injury.

In answer to the question: GET TO KNOW YOURSELF FIRST. BE SURE YOU KNOW WHAT IT IS YOU ACTUALLY DESIRE. The indications are that present relationships—the ones you are asking about—are based to a great degree on wishful thinking.

Illusion is the keynote. The answer to this question is favorable if the subject happens to be in the film business, as producer, actor, writer, etc. Or if he is associated with television—the visual arts. Otherwise, the indications are that this question is based upon dreamlike qualities which, however beautiful, have nothing to do with practical living.

Avoid signing contracts. Remember, if you are asking

about an individual, he may be well-intentioned—but he does NOT appear to be for you.

The number 7 symbol, as an indicator of your question, reveals that you are concerned with a person, or situation; the relationship does not seem destined to last.

Learn everything you can while it does continue. Then, get off alone. You have a lot to learn about yourself.

IF THE TOTAL IS 8:

The question here concerns money matters, responsibility, perhaps marriage; emphasis certainly seems to lie on finance and concern over finances due to added pressure, responsibility and an additional mouth to feed.

Birth signs involved are Capricorn and Cancer.

The subject, dialing 8 as an indicator for a direct question, is asking about business matters and is concerned about authority, responsibility and the money to run things as he would like to, or has been ordered to: number 8 is this kind of symbol and has much to do with standing in the community and with AMBITION.

The answer, generally, is YES. Accept added responsibility, because there is no constructive way to avoid it. The answer, too, is *no,* in that this project will be no bed of roses. THERE IS WORK TO BE DONE AND NOW IS THE TIME TO ACCEPT AND MEET A CHALLENGE.

Commercial enterprises are favored only if the subject realizes the necessity of WORK and INVESTMENT. Nothing halfway will do here. There is no putting one foot in the water to see if it is cold. It is all the way or nothing at all.

In matters of a personal nature, there is no experimenting, no hitting and running. ONCE THE SUBJECT BECOMES INVOLVED HERE, IT IS ALL THE WAY, probably marriage or children, or both.

In matters of a business nature—the same applies. Losses are incurred unless the subject is prepared to devote FULL TIME to the project.

YES, do invest. YES, do marry and get engaged or continue the romance. YES, do these things—*if you are mature enough to face a big challenge and to face a battle without running for cover.*

The question or problem being thought of here is of a serious nature. If the subject is not *consciously* aware of this fact, his *subconscious* most decidedly is and is trying (through the Thought Dial) to tell him so.

Build, invest, advertise, let loved ones know you care.

Sex, in a creative, mature sense, plays an important role here.

The answer to the question is WORK.

The subject will meet with emotional and professional failure unless he is willing to WORK.

IF THE TOTAL IS 9:

A relationship, a cycle, much of the recent past—is coming to an end—and the answer to the question is BREAK AWAY FROM THE OLD AND TAKE THE ROAD TOWARD A NEW DIRECTION AND LIFE.

Yes, be willing to break off.

Yes, you are right in sensing you have been carrying another's rightful responsibility.

Yes, be a humanitarian and a nurse and a teacher and lend a helping hand—but DRAW THE LINE AT BEING "USED," AT BEING TAKEN ADVANTAGE OF BY PERSONS WHO ARE IN THE HABIT OF HAVING YOU DO THE UNPLEASANT TASKS.

Birth signs involved are Aries and Libra.

In answer to this question: Past association, partnerships—business and personal—have outlived their usefulness. A NEW APPROACH is required here. Proper perspective is being called for by the subconscious via this symbol.

Direct, independent, forceful action is required on the part of the subject. Otherwise, he will be unhappy, he will lag behind, he will lose much in both a professional and a personal sense.

A RELATIONSHIP IS TERMINATING. It is NOT beginning, no matter how things appear on the surface (to the conscious mind). The subconscious clearly states that an influence is fading out of the subject's life. Fresh, original ideas are needed here.

This is the time, in relation to this particular question, to ADVERTISE, to let many (instead of a few) know of your capabilities. GOOD PUBLIC RELATIONS ARE ESSENTIAL FOR A SUCCESSFUL OUTCOME OF THIS PROBLEM.

Generally, the answer is in the affirmative. Specifically, BREAK FROM THE OLD—take the initiative and LEAD THE WAY. Try something NEW!

To successfully resolve this question, insist on originality and let others carry their own load.

IF THE TOTAL IS 11:

Birth signs involved are AQUARIUS and LEO, CANCER and CAPRICORN.

IN ANSWER TO THE QUESTION: Trust your intuition!

Intuitive intellect is required here. No outsider can provide the right advice, no matter how logical that counsel may appear. The subconscious, by delivering this symbol, is asking to take over. The problem here is one involving EMOTIONS. As such, application and consideration of PURELY FACTUAL material is not apt to be of much aid.

Best advice, in relation to your question: BE IDEALISTIC. Stick to your ideals. Do not lower your sights. Refuse to be influenced by those who, however well-meaning, try to get you to be "practical." What they actually mean, is "practical" through their eyes, the way they see the question. WHATEVER YOUR SUBCONSCIOUS TELLS YOU IS FOR YOUR BENEFIT, THAT IS OF IMPORTANCE HERE.

An affair of the heart seems to be involved in this question. What is to be avoided is an attitude that leads to brooding, to depression and defeatism. IF NECESSARY, MAKE A SUDDEN MOVE: put your cards on the table and call the bluff!

Eventually, as this problem is resolved, YOU WILL BE THE TEACHER. Your advice will be followed. There is reluctance—on the surface. BUT YOU CAN WIN OUT. Keep this thought in mind. It is one your subconscious is attempting to filter through to your conscious mind. Be AWARE of your potential.

A child may be involved, or those who are dependent upon the subject. These considerations are important, and the subject should follow his heart in this matter. ANY OTHER WAY LEADS TO UNHAPPINESS.

The answer is generally negative, but ONLY IN A TEMPORARY SENSE. By hanging on, and remaining true to INTUITION and IDEALS, the subject eventually wins.

IF THE TOTAL IS 22:

Birth signs involved in this question are SCORPIO and TAURUS.

In answer to the question: CREATIVITY AND A SENSE OF "BUILDING" ARE ALL-IMPORTANT.

Although the answer is generally negative, the FINAL outcome is of a POSITIVE nature.

This appears contradictory on the surface. But in reality it is simply a matter of OVERCOMING ROUTINE OBSTACLES and getting down to work on CREATIVE projects.

The subconscious, in offering this "master symbol,"

clearly indicates that the subject need worry *only as long as he remains bogged down with feelings of insecurity*.

Yes, now is the time to BUILD.

NO, now is not the time to go back over details, to be disturbed by associates who are dominated by the petty, the inconsequential.

YES, tear down in order to REBUILD.

NO, do not let others talk you into a "smaller investment."

YES, do see the project (possibilities for the future) as a whole.

HAVE VISION!

Vision will provide needed confidence. Sure, the task, the ideal is huge in scope: BUT THE SUBJECT IS CAPABLE OF COMING UP WITH THE RIGHT ANSWERS (talent and creative ability and hard work).

Money may be forthcoming from a marriage or business partner.

Inspiration depends upon the subject's FREEDOM. Thus he should not allow himself to be tied down by promises of economy.

Refuse to budge if an idea must crumple as a result.

THE FUTURE HOLDS A SMILE FOR THE SUBJECT. He should give it a chance to show!

10
Yes and No Technique

This section is inspired by Dr. Marc Edmund Jones' superb reference work on horary astrology,* in which Dr. Jones discusses the "yes and no technique" in interpreting horary charts. I consider that technique invaluable. It gets to the essence of horary astrology, the very purpose for its existence: to provide direct, concise answers to specific questions.

* Llewellyn Publications, Ltd., Los Angeles.

This technique, utilized in connection with the Thought Dial, should be looked upon in the proper perspective. It is like the light provided from a match as compared to a shining electric bulb. The flare of the match enables the subject to get his bearings, so to speak. The match is the yes and no technique as applied to the Thought Dial. However, for prolonged light, the section "Your Subconscious Thoughts" and "Direct Questions Answered" are necessary.

Thus for so-called minor questions, or quick insights, the yes and no technique is valid.

The subject thinks of a question with a yes or no answer, then dials three numbers, reducing the total to a single number (unless the total happens to add to 11 or 22).

IF THE TOTAL IS 1:
YES—definite.

IF THE TOTAL IS 2:
NO—definite.

IF THE TOTAL IS 3:
YES—less definite.

IF THE TOTAL IS 4:
NO—less definite.

IF THE TOTAL IS 5:
YES—Definite.

IF THE TOTAL IS 6:
NO—definite.

IF THE TOTAL IS 7:
NO—but a yes is indicated after some delay.

IF THE TOTAL IS 8:
NO—but a yes is soon indicated.

IF THE TOTAL IS 9:
YES—but along different lines. New ideas needed.

IF THE TOTAL IS 11:
NO—but something better is forthcoming.

IF THE TOTAL IS 22:
YES—definite.

11
Locating Lost Articles

This section, as well as the next, "Picking Winners," must rightfully be categorized as speculative. That is, speculative in relation to the previous parts of this work. Through the research that has ensued, it is felt that "Your Subconscious Thoughts," "Direct Questions Answered" and "Yes and No Technique" are more than speculative. The material contained in those sections is presented as work that has been tested and which has yielded promising results—results, in most cases, as satisfactory as any astrological or general psychological technique. Admittedly, additional research is required before we know what it is we have here in the Thought Dial. The same is true of any technique dealing with human beings, their actions and reactions, particularly their thoughts—and, more specifically, their *inner* thoughts. That is why this volume is being released at this time. I have gone as far as I can—alone. It is with certainty that I state that further experiments, performed by those in possession of this work, will enlighten us to a greater degree—perhaps beyond our most optimistic expectations.

That is why it is necessary to differentiate between what has gone forth and what is now being presented. The *theory* is basically the same. Nothing is "lost." The subconscious, or some part of our selves, *knows* where the object has been placed (or misplaced): *or whether the object is not to be found by the subject*. This technique has been utilized in horary astrology. It has been used, too, in connection with numbers. I am indebted to Sepharial and his work *The Kabala of Numbers** for much of the information provided here.

* David McKay Company, New York, 1945.

INSTRUCTIONS: Subject thinks of the object he wishes to locate: when a clear picture of the object is obtained, or when the question "Where is it?" is formed, three numbers are dialed on the Thought Dial. As in previous instances, the numbers (with the exception of 11 and 22) are reduced to a single digit between 1 and 9.

IF THE TOTAL IS 1:

The object is, most likely, in a main part of a house: the living room or bedroom. Sepharial suggests that it may well be found in a room near white linen. He recommends, too, that a fair child be questioned.

Direction: SOUTH.

It would appear† that the object was lost while the subject (or whoever *did* lose it) was in pursuit of pleasure: a hunting trip, a picnic, etc. It would appear that the object *will* be found.

IF THE TOTAL IS 2:

Specifically, Sepharial declares the object is to be found in a house, in a vase or bowl, or close by. Indications are that someone will aid in finding the thing lost, perhaps a maid or housekeeper, or a cook.

Direction: SOUTH.

The object lost *will* be found.

IF THE TOTAL IS 3:

The object being sought may be located in a passage or between papers. It could well be found in a place where men congregate.

Direction: NORTH.

Indications are that carelessness was involved in this loss, not necessarily carelessness on the part of the subject— but on the part of the one he trusts.

The general indication is that the article will be found.

IF THE TOTAL IS 4:

For this total, Serpharial states, "The article is in your possession, and is not lost."

Assuming, however, that the article is *not* in the subject's possession, the direction is likely to be toward the NORTHEAST. Indications are that the article will be recovered.

It would appear, from this total on the Thought Dial, that the object has been misplaced due to absent-

† Besides material provided by Sepharial, reference is made here, as with other symbols, to rules set forth by William Lilly, in 1647, in his classic work, *Lilly's Introduction to Astrology.*

mindedness on the part of the subject. A number of other details appear to occupy his attention—then, bolt-like—he remembers a series of events which lead to recovery of the lost object.

IF THE TOTAL IS 5:

Sepharial suggests, "Look under a hat, turban, or other headgear." The indications are that the object *will* be found—*once the subject stops looking*.

Direction: Toward the WEST.

It appears that the object was lost while the subject was in transit: travel, communications—perhaps the mailing of a letter—all might be involved here.

IF THE TOTAL IS 6:

The object, according to Sepharial, might be found where sandals or boots are kept. The possibility is strong that the thing being sought is on a shelf, or a stand of some kind.

The direction is either to the extreme EAST or WEST.

The odds of finding this lost object are *not* great.

IF THE TOTAL IS 7:

Sepharial specifically states, "Ask your servant, a maid especially connected with the wardrobe."

The direction is EAST.

The indications are that the object will *not* be found. It is most likely in a place associated with water. There is deception indicated here, indicative of the fact that someone is withholding information, thus lessening the odds of recovering what is lost.

IF THE TOTAL IS 8:

Someone else may find this, but it is *not* likely the subject will be directly responsible. Sepharial states the lost object may be on a shelf or horizontal ledge.

The direction is NORTH.

Illness of some sort (specifically a cold or ailment affecting the bones) appears to be connected with this loss.

The object may be in a field, possibly where cattle graze.

IF THE TOTAL IS 9:

According to Sepharial: "A child has it among some clothing." The indications are that the object *will* be recovered.

The direction is EAST.

This object may have been lost due to a quarrel. That

is, the subject—in a state of anger or excitement—unknowingly discarded it, perhaps in a fire, where it was subsequently recovered by a young person.

IF THE TOTAL IS 11:

Quoting Sepharial: "You must take a short journey to a tank, pool, or stretch of water."

The direction is NORTHEAST.

It would appear that this object was lost at a resort, or where people go to relax: a swimming pool, a nightclub, perhaps a private party.

Much effort will have to be exerted if this object is to be recovered.

The manner in which it was lost might prove embarrassing; the subject may wish to forget the matter.

IF THE TOTAL IS 22:

Sepharial states flatly, "The thing is on a shelf in the house, and will be speedily found."

The direction is WEST.

Indications are that it *will* be found.

The kitchen or bathroom would appear to be the site.

The subject should avoid hasty conclusions or accusations.

12

Picking Winners

Ben Hunter, who conducted a "Night Owl" radio program in Los Angeles, tested the Thought Dial on the air. He selected three numbers which, when added and reduced to a single digit, equaled 1. Number 1, of course, is associated with the Sun. First, as Matt Weinstock reported in his newspaper column, Ben had concentrated on *winning* at the track. He had the thought clearly formed in his mind when he selected three numbers. Since the numbers added to 1 (all double numbers, with the exception of 11 and 22, are reduced to a single digit between 1 and 9), he was told to select horses whose names reminded *him*, or suggested to *him*, the *symbols* of number 1: the Sun, pioneer, new starts, originality, creativity, etc. Number 1, being associated with the Sun, is also related to the zodiacal sign of Leo (especially good for speculation, being the natural fifth sign in the zodiac), and so names related to that sign would also have been significant.

It would be too much to hope for the kind of success Ben Hunter obtained in picking winners with the Thought Dial. However, there is reason to believe that, through use of the Thought Dial (free utilization of "subconscious knowledge"), the average of winners will be greater. Anecdotes about persons who are able to "win on paper" but not when they are actually betting money at the track, are numerous—too numerous to be mere coincidences. There is a pattern in stories of persons who are able to predict the outcome of a football game, or a race-track competition, or other event, but who, when it comes to picking winners with cash on the line, freeze up or allow themselves to be touted off their original selections. Why does this happen?

It happens, in all probability, because the conscious or censor mind stands in the way when pressure is applied; there is too much rationalizing, too much thinking, or what passes for thinking and what, in all likelihood, is a "pinching off" of the flow from the subconscious. In other words, sitting at home with his newspaper list of competitors, a man is able to relax (knowing he is not going to risk money, anyway) and choose. The same man, whose average is high on paper, loses his canny sense once his own money is on the line at the track. This is because he is too conscious of what he is doing; he is trying to be logical and, perhaps, logic is a detriment in this sort of thing. Detriment or not, it would appear (as in the striking example of Ben Hunter's success) that once the subject is relaxed enough, or "unaware enough," his subconscious makes itself felt and he fares better.

This boils down to the theory that the subconscious is able to *perceive* the future or is *aware* of it: it is the case of the "time line" once more, with the supposition that the subconscious is able to see the beginning, middle and end of it. If we will only let it!

Dr. Rhine, I am sure, would attribute this "ability to see" to extrasensory perception. Specifically, he would term this section an experiment in *precognition*. That is, the ability to "recognize" a future event before it occurs. Dr. Rhine may be right. The subconscious may, after all, have nothing whatever to do with foretelling the future. But, then again, there may be more of an association between the subconscious and ESP than any of us know. The point here is that no matter *why* or *how* the Thought Dial works, the important thing is that it *does*. So, in the long run, it does not matter (for our purposes) whether the symbols are presented to us by the subconscious or by ESP. What *does* matter is that, through the Thought Dial, *some* element within ourselves is tapped, and we are thus able to "see" more.

In picking winners, the subject concentrates on the *outcome* of the contest. If it is a horse race, he should think of collecting money at the end of the race: he must picture himself at the parimutuel window, holding a winning ticket. With this thought clearly in mind, he dials three numbers and, in the usual manner, reduces the total to a single number between 1 and 9 (with the exceptions of 11 and 22, the only double numbers retained as totals).

The symbols represented by the total dialed provide the winners. It needn't be a horse race. The process of "picking winners" with the Thought Dial can be applied to boxing matches, football or baseball games, perhaps even political contests! If the Thought Dial comes up with an individual's zodiacal sign—then pick that person, by all means! That is, if in a boxing match one fighter was born under Capricorn, another under Cancer, and the Thought Dial total was 8, then the Capricorn boxer would be selected (number 8 associated with Saturn; and that planet rules Capricorn).

An explanation of how the Thought Dial, on occasion, reveals birth dates of individuals is provided in the section "Direct Questions Answered."

All right, we're ready now for the symbols associated with various Thought Dial totals. The list provided here is by no means complete. It is hoped that readers, upon experimenting, will develop key words of their own.

Reminder: Think of yourself as having picked the winner: the contest or competition is over, and you have chosen the right animal, athlete, political candidate, etc. With this thought clearly in mind, start dialing.

IF THE TOTAL IS 1:

Number 1 is associated with the Sun and the zodiacal sign of Leo the Lion.

Key words: SUN, INDEPENDENCE, LEADER, ORIGINALITY, SPECULATION, LOVE, THEATER, BELLE OF THE BALL, EGO, CHILDREN AND ANYTHING NEW, STARTLING OR SEXY.

This number, in picking winners, is considered fortunate.

IF THE TOTAL IS 2:

Number 2 is associated with the Moon and the zodiacal sign of Cancer the Crab.

Key words: MOON, BROODING, HOME, SECURITY, THE WOMAN IN YOUR LIFE, MOTHER, INSANITY, THE PUBLIC, PATRIOTISM, COMFORT, DIPLOMACY AND ANYTHING ASSOCIATED WITH A SENSE OF SAFETY AS PROVIDED BY PARENTS OR HOME.

This number, in picking winners, is *not* as fortunate as some others.

IF THE TOTAL IS 3:

Number 3 is associated with the planet Jupiter and the zodiacal sign of Sagittarius the Archer.

Key words: LUCK, EXPANSION, MONEY, EXTRAVAGANCE, OBESITY, PLENTIFUL, FORTUNE, PHILOSOPHY, LONG JOURNEYS, RELIGION, NOBILITY, HIGH-MINDEDNESS, FRANKNESS AND ANYTHING LARGE IN A PHYSICAL SENSE OR EXPANSIVE IN ANY MANNER.

This number, in picking winners, is considered fortunate.

IF THE TOTAL IS 4:

Number 4 is associated with the planet Uranus and with the zodiacal sign of Aquarius the Water Bearer.

Key words: ELECTRICITY, RESTRICTION, FRIENDS, WISHES, TELEVISION, AVIATION, MAGNETISM, GRAVITY, ASTROLOGY, STRENGTH, SQUARE, DETAILS, METHODS, FULFILLMENT, TEST AND ANYTHING ASSOCIATED WITH FULFILLMENT OF WISHES BASED ON HARD WORK.

This number, in picking winners, is *not* as fortunate as some others.

IF THE TOTAL IS 5:

Number 5 is associated with the planet Mercury and with the zodiacal signs of Gemini the Twins and Virgo the Virgin.

Key words: INVESTIGATION, COMMUNICATION, MEMBERS OF THE OPPOSITE SEX, LOVE, ADVENTURE, CHANGE, TRAVEL, VARIETY, DETECTIVES, SHORT JOURNEYS, DISCRIM-

INATION, SERVANTS, JOB, BROTHERS AND SISTERS, AFFAIR OF THE HEART, MARRIAGE AND ANYTHING ASSOCIATED WITH CREATIVE ACTIVITY.

This number, in picking winners, is considered fortunate.

IF THE TOTAL IS 6:

Number 6 is associated with the planet Venus and with the zodiacal signs of Taurus the Bull and Libra the Scales.

Key words: HOME, LOVED ONES, FAMILY, CHANGE OF RESIDENCE, DOMESTICITY, VOICE, LUXURY, LAZINESS, COLLECTING, MONEY, JUSTICE, LEGAL CONTRACTS, HOBBIES ASSOCIATED WITH THE ACCUMULATION OF OBJECTS, SUCH AS COINS, STAMPS, PAINTINGS ETC., TRANQUILLITY, PEACE AND ANYTHING ASSOCIATED WITH HOME AND FAMILY, OR WITH THE VOICE AND SECURITY.

This number, in picking winners, is *not* as fortunate as some others.

IF THE TOTAL IS 7:

Number 7 is associated with the planet Neptune and the zodiacal sign of Pisces the Fish.

Key words: DECEPTION, PARTNERS, INSTITUTIONS SUCH AS PRISONS, HOSPITALS, ORPHANAGES, ETC., ILLUSION, NONREALITY, WATER, MOTION PICTURES, TELEVISION, AN "UNSEEN AUDIENCE," PSYCHIC PHENOMENA, MEDIUMS, EXTRASENSORY PERCEPTION, SPIRITUALISM, OR ANYTHING ASSOCIATED WITH INFLUENCES THAT CAN BE FELT BUT NOT SEEN.

This number, in picking winners, is either *very good* or *unfortunate in the extreme.*

IF THE TOTAL IS 8:

Number 8 is associated with the planet Saturn and the zodiacal sign of Capricorn the Goat.

Key words: MONEY POWER, RESPONSIBILITY, COMMERCIAL SUCCESS, MARRIAGE, SEX, CREATIVITY, CONCEPTION, PREGNANCY, STANDING IN THE COMMUNITY, AMBITION, ASPIRATIONS, AUTHORITY, THE PAST, BONES, AND ANYTHING ASSOCIATED WITH CAREER, DECAY OR BUSINESS.

This number, in picking winners, is considered fortunate.

IF THE TOTAL IS 9:

Number 9 is associated with the planet Mars and the zodiacal sign of Aries the Ram.

Key words: UNIVERSAL APPEAL, ADVERTISING, PUBLIC RELATIONS, PUBLISHING, NURSING, SYMPATHY, CONSIDER-

ATION, FAME, RECOGNITION, HOSPITALS, PERSONALITY, WAR AND PEACE AND ANYTHING ASSOCIATED WITH POETRY, SYMBOLISM, WORLD-WIDE PUBLICATIONS.

This number, in picking winners, is considered fortunate.

IF THE TOTAL IS 11:

Number 11 is associated with the planet Uranus and the zodiacal sign of Aquarius the Water Bearer.

Key words: INTUITION, OCCULT, TEACHER, WRITER, INSTRUCTOR, PREDICTION, HELP FROM FRIENDS, POWER, ADVENTURE, ENERGY FROM UNKNOWN SOURCES, SACRED, LIBERTY, BRAVERY, UNDERSTANDING, RELIGION AND ANYTHING ASSOCIATED WITH PHILOSOPHY AND FAITH.

This number, in picking winners, is considered fortunate.

IF THE TOTAL IS 22:

Number 22 is associated with the planet Pluto and the zodiacal sign of Scorpio the Scorpion.

Key words: MASTER, BUILDER, BRILLIANCE, FUTURE, IDEALS, ALTRUISM, ORGANIZATION, COMMUNITY, MONEY OBTAINED FROM PARTNERS, EXPRESSION, MESSENGER, TEARING DOWN IN ORDER TO REBUILD, THINGS HIDDEN AND ANYTHING ASSOCIATED WITH COMPLETION OR UTOPIA.

This number, in picking winners, is considered fortunate.

13

Further Examination

Man, as we have indicated, did not invent numbers; he *discovered* them. Indeed, before the advent of man, Nature apparently made use of number and symbol. In effect, man came along and learned to follow Nature's example.

Lawrence Lipton is a poet and scholar of Venice, California. His work has appeared in numerous influential publications in this country and abroad; his opinions and essays—often of a controversial nature—are quoted and reprinted. His challenging concepts have appeared in *Life, Chicago Review, The Nation, The London Magazine, Arizona Quarterly* and *The Atlantic,* among other publications. Commenting on the Thought Dial, and its use of symbols, Lipton states:

"I suspect that what you have here is a *mantram,* which is what the Buddhists would call it. A *mantram* is an object which, in itself, is a symbol, *something which sets off or triggers the numinous* experience of the individual, so that he becomes, for the moment, a receptor for whatever truth he is seeking. That truth may be a desire to understand the future or to relive the past. It may be a desire to understand the inner workings of his own psyche. It may be a desire to know whether he should marry, or go into business for himself, or whatever it is he is trying to do or understand. The Thought Dial becomes for him a *mantram* which triggers the mechanism. And it is as valid as the user or subject can make it. Any *mantram,* in this sense, is limited in its value to what the user or subject can make of it. All symbols are metaphors. And metaphors are interpreted by the individual within the scope of his own understanding."

Lipton goes on to say:

"All views of the world and the universe are human-mental in concept. In order to communicate these concepts we use number and symbol. I suspect these symbols are *not* confined to human life. Animals use number and symbol. The bees, for example, are known to use language which certainly consists of number and symbol. Writer Gerald Heard has written extensively of this—bees being able to communicate to each other regarding the location and sources of nectar supply. Bees are known to move to the left, right, up and down, a certain number of motions creating a map, enabling them to communicate with other bees in the hive. So, you see, symbols are not limited to man. The entire universe is alive, is articulate and communicates. The line between the numerology of crystals to the mathematics of Einstein is only a matter of degree."

Lipton, whose scholarship is respected among writers and intellectuals, continues:

"The whole universe is based upon number. This, of

course, has been known for a long time. It was known to Pythagoras and others. Number is language. Language never had a beginning. It is as old as life is, at both ends of the scale—past and present. Communication implies symbol. The language of the chromosome, for example—I speak of it as a language because the communication which takes place between the cells and the growth apparatus in the single cell and the multiplying cell—is arranged very much as a script might be.

"Much of man's knowledge of number comes from the *Kabala*. The *Kabala*, historically, represents a rather late attempt to rediscover the mystery of numbers in relation to human conduct. The *Kabala*, if read with an eye to metaphor rather than to strict mathematics, can be understood. It is to be read in the same way Jung has re-read astrology and alchemy. Ultimately, all mathematical symbols are reducible to metaphor. . . .

"The *Kabala* was passed on orally for a long time, going back perhaps to the Alexandrian Jews, who were influenced by the Hermetic teachings of the Greek gnostic and Neo-platonic cults. One of its principal sources is the *Zohar*, which the 13th century scholar Moses de Leon attributed to Simon ben Yochai, a great scholar of the 2nd century. The greatest influence of the *Kabala*, on both Jews and Christians, dates from the 7th century onwards in Europe, undergoing corruption from century to century as its meanings became clouded by ignorance and exploitation by charlatans."

Lipton concludes by saying:

"In Hebrew legend, God created the world by *number*. He did this by means of an alphabet, which appeared in letters of fire above his crown. *Every letter has a number*. Hebrews, like Greeks, *use letters to denote number*, as well as alphabetical or phonetic sign.

"All symbols, including the symbols on the Thought Dial, have a relationship to our needs. Anything that exists in the universe, anything that is conceivable, has a past, present and future. In a real sense the past and present and future exist simultaneously. Every now and then some persons obtain an inkling of eternity. Animals appear to have the faculty of seeing the past, present and future as one. Some animals can predict weather and thus prepare themselves, for example, with a thick coat. The eye is formed in embryo before there is any need for sight. Does the embryo know it is going to need an eye when born?

"Yes, it appears that Nature has prepared a script, one that is built into each organism, making it prophetic, enabling it to see beyond the present and into the future. If this is true in Nature—objects appearing before their purpose has become a reality—then there is no reason why the human mind cannot also conceive of the future. If it is possible for a hedgehog, it is certainly possible for a human being."

14
Sound and Color

Numbers, as symbols, are related to *sounds* and *colors* as well as to planets and thoughts.

Here the numbers are being presented as they relate to sound and color. As Lipton declares, it is up to the user to get what he can from this relationship. Perhaps the *color* relationship will prove helpful in association with the section "Picking Winners," or in relation to "Locating Lost Articles." I leave that to the individual. More experiment is required.

As for *sound,* perhaps some students will evolve a method of utilizing the Thought Dial to *depict names,* just as it now can be used to perceive zodiacal signs. This, of course, remains to be seen.

I present the Thought Dial symbols in relation to *sound* and *color* in the spirit of experiment. I will, as in all instances, be most anxious to hear from students regarding their experiments with this section.

NUMBER ONE:
  Color: orange, gold.
  Sound: A and I and the consonants M, D, T.
NUMBER TWO:
  Color: green.

Sound: B, P, F, V.

NUMBER THREE:

Color: violet, purple.

Sound: related to all palatals, as Ch, J and soft G.

NUMBER FOUR:

Color: gray, black and white (stripes).

Sound: C.

NUMBER FIVE:

Color: yellow, pink.

Sound: E, H, N.

NUMBER SIX:

Color: primrose, turquoise, pale blue.

Sound: O, U, W.

NUMBER SEVEN:

Color: Lavender, lilac, heliotrope.

Sound: similar to 2: B, P, F, V.

NUMBER EIGHT:

Color: indigo, dark blue, chocolate, black.

Sound: S, Sh, Z.

NUMBER NINE:

Color: red, scarlet, crimson.

Sound: K, hard G, R.

NUMBER ELEVEN:

Color: similar to 4: gray, black and white (stripes).

Sound: similar to 4: C.

NUMBER TWENTY-TWO:

Color: red and black.

Sound: S, K, G, R.

Part TWO

15

Love

The interpretations that follow are based on recent tests; the core of the meanings are provided and are purposely presented in a relatively light vein. As in other sections of *Thought Dial*, it is up to the operator to add dimension as he gains skill and insight. TOTALS:

ONE—For you, love is romance! It is a new world, a world almost detached from the one in which you are now living. Your subconscious reactions show that you are sincere, that you are looking for the "one person," and that when you find him (or her) there will be plenty of love. What you must avoid is an attitude of selfishness, which exhibits itself occasionally and which would not be at all satisfactory in connection with love.

TWO—Love, or the thought of it, often depresses you. You are not fond of chasing or being chased. You prefer security and the sanity of a steady routine. Love, for you, represents maturity: a home of your own, a family, children upon whom you can shower your affection. Your attitude is stable, commendable. But, remember, in order to find love, you must seek it! Prince (or Princess) Charming is not likely to appear out of nowhere. Which means you must avoid getting into a rut in either your attitudes or actions.

THREE—"Frivolous" is the word for your attitude toward love. At least that's true for the present. Love, according to your projective psychology total, represents a gay social whirl. And you are not at all anxious to settle down. You prefer to look over the field. That's fine, perhaps even commendable at this time. But, later, as you grow older, more sure of yourself and what you are seeking in a life partner, this will change. You will become more selective. But for now—have fun! Wholesome contacts with members of the opposite sex will help solidify your ideas of love.

FOUR—Love, for you, is friendship intensified, which is not bad, not bad at all. It represents—this projective psychological total—a grown-up attitude toward emotional well-being. Your attitude is one of steadiness. You are not one to run hither and yon—rather, you prefer loyalty. You will find that you are most likely to be attracted to those who exhibit qualities of thrift, steadfastness and sincerity.

FIVE—For you, love means family: it means children and also physical and mental attractiveness. Your attitude is based on a combination of the family unit and romance with a capital "R"! You feel, according to this test, that you will travel in connection with love. Perhaps your thoughts are concentrated on education, college—for the test total shows that love means learning to you. Higher learning. Which, in a sense, is what LOVE is!

SIX—Domesticity is your key note in connection with love. Your subconscious attitude is one of home, family and a sweet, considerate mate. It would appear, from this total, that you possess qualities of maturity worthy of the wisest adult. On this, congratulations! Your love life should be rich and full. And it's a good bet you'll have a home picked out before taking any steps down the aisle. Your attitude, your thoughts concerning love, are practical and reasonable.

SEVEN—Why do you have such a long face when you think about love? It can be fun, you know. As a matter of fact, it should be. Finding the right person, sharing your life with one you love, represents fulfillment of man's fondest wish. Your total, however, reveals that you have misgivings. On the positive side, this is fine; it makes you selective, discriminating. But, negatively, it could represent an attitude best described as "too fussy." Loosen up! Combine good taste and discrimination with an open mind —and heart.

EIGHT—Love and money make a wonderful combination, and this takes the words right out of your mouth. You think of love as the most important thing in your life. You are certainly as romantic as the next person, perhaps more so. However, your projective number total reveals that you tie in money with a happy love life. There is nothing wrong in doing so. But emotional maturity dictates that you acquire a sense of proportion. Life consists of love, material possessions—and lots of other things, too. Think it over—carefully.

NINE—Your sense of love is universal! That is, you associate love with generosity, well-being, with world peace, with idealism put into practice. This is commendable. Your projective number total reveals that you could never be happy with a person who was cruel or selfish, or self-centered. Your own nature appears to be outgoing; your goals are altruistic. When you find love—you will be finding life!

ELEVEN—When it comes to love, your ideas are apt to be considered "unconventional." Love, for you, means reaching up to, and entering, a new realm. The Thought Dial total here is indicative of a person who regards love as almost fatalistic: there are occult or "destiny" implications—it is almost as if you are convinced the matter is out of your hands. There are two extremes here, one positive and the other negative. On the positive side, your attitude toward love is mature in that you are not seeking perfection. On the negative side, you are so "destiny-minded" about love that you are completely passive: you wait and wait for your love to come riding up on a white charger.

TWENTY-TWO—Love means power here: the power of a life-providing force. You are idealistic, perhaps to a fault, in your attitude toward this emotion. Your job is to arrive at a definition of terms within yourself. There is no room for confusion, which means you cannot afford to delay a process of intensive self-analysis in connection with LOVE. Love, for you, is likely to mean beauty, but also problems involving PHYSICAL relations with members of the opposite sex. Greater happiness is indicated when you overcome rigid or fixed attitudes.

16

Money

Let us experiment, at this time, with a new *operating* technique. We have already stated that the actual Thought Dial is a *mantram*, a procedure, a method of "drawing out" numerical aspects of the subconscious. Now, for the following tests, we temporarily eliminate the dial. Understand, the dial *can* be used here, or *eliminated*, as the operator prefers.

Much of this material was prepared for the national magazine *Teen* and the interpretations are aimed at adolescents.

I am reproducing this material *almost* as it appeared in order to stimulate *desire for experiment* within readers. It is my point that processes of Thought Dial are limitless: what this eventually will come to mean to the future is a matter of *exciting conjecture*. How soon final conclusions are arrived at depends upon this type of variation and experiment.

Here we will read interpretations purposely aimed at young persons: but the kernel of general or overall meaning is contained and will enable the student to add material and to verify past definitions.

Psychologists say humans are very much interested in three things—in the following order: LOVE, MONEY and HEALTH.

Through our instantaneous number-selection technique, we have already examined YOUR reaction (what you *really* think) to love. Now, let's explore your subconscious attitude toward MONEY.

All of us, whether poetic or materialistic, are living in a civilization where money has assumed tremendous import. We are not saying this is right or wrong. But it exists, and insight into *your* subconscious attitude toward money may

84

help you both now and when you assume the responsibilities that accompany adulthood.

Our test is simple. Concentrate on the word "money." Then check or circle any of the three numbers in our table below:

1	2	3
4	5	6
7	8	9
	11	22

Now, add your numbers from left to right until you arrive at a single total between 1 and 9. For example, suppose you select 4, 2 and 7. Adding, the total is 13. Now, adding 13, we arrive at 1 plus 3, or a final answer of 4. Retain only 11 and 22 as double numbers.

Use this psychological technique to test your own subconscious reaction to MONEY. Simply concentrate on the word, then select any of the three numbers provided. Then add from left to right until you arrive at a single-digit total. When you do, check below for your inner thoughts concerning MONEY.

If your total is ONE: Money, in itself, is not particularly impressive as far as you are concerned. What *does* impress you is the *manner* in which money is obtained. You gain pleasure from finances only if the gaining of income comes about through inventiveness, originality and pioneering action. You will gain most through your own creative efforts and by your ability to attract those who, in turn, seem able to attract money. Your subconscious reaction to money is, "I like it, but it is by no means everything." In other words, you are an idealist and rate LOVE over money.

If your total is TWO you are indifferent to money. It would indeed be difficult to *buy* you. You have to be won over. You judge neither yourself nor others by financial standards. Money, according to your subconscious reaction, represents SECURITY, especially in connection with the home, family and children. But, as an end in itself, money is very likely to leave you cold. You can gain financial independence by being diplomatic; you lose out if you attempt to force issues. You are mature and serene about your financial affairs.

If your total is THREE your subconscious reaction reveals that you are apt to associate MONEY with LUCK. And who can say? Maybe you're right. However, this instantaneous number-selection total indicates that you tend toward extravagance. In some ways this can be a charming characteristic. But in other ways it is not only impractical but downright dangerous. Try to consider the feelings of others where money is concerned. Impoverished or insolvent people won't be amused by your flippancy.

If your total is FOUR your attitude toward money is likely to be quite sober. This is commendable. You know the value of money and are willing to work hard in order to gain financial security. However, there is a tendency for you to become gloomy and moody, to brood over whether you have enough. Brooding will get you nowhere. Remember, what counts is doing your best; the rewards (financial and otherwise) will follow. It is good to be economical and practical, but not to the point where you become a tightwad. Success is shown, but you have to work for what you get. No one is going to be giving things away, at least not to you.

If your total is FIVE it reveals that very often you associate money with TRAVEL. And with romance! Money, at its best, represents (to you) change, travel, variety, affairs of the heart. This may be a misconception; others will tell you that your attitude will change as you grow older. They may be right, these well-meaning persons, where they themselves are concerned. But your thoughts, your attitude, your feelings are right for you. Now, how to go about becoming financially secure? Well, your number total would indicate that you gain through communication, through writing, self-expression, acting and other creative endeavors—or through the selling of creative efforts. Book publishing, authors' agent, syndicate-feature selling—these might appeal to you. Anyway, the odds are that you will have money, and romance!

If your total is SIX, money often means HARMONY to you. In other words, you associate an abundance of cash with the erasure of worry or friction. Who is to say you are wrong? Subconsciously, money is a necessity to you where marriage, travel or adventure is concerned. You are not a fanatic about money, but you have a practical, mature view toward it. You associate money with family, with the ability to help loved ones.

If your total is SEVEN you are not at all sure of yourself when it comes to money. There is a tendency, revealed here, for you to regard wealth with a certain awe and questioning. Where does it come from? Where does it go? You should try to be more down-to-earth where finances are concerned. Draw up a budget and follow it. You have a tendency to be improvident. You vacillate between free-spending and niggardly behavior. This total would suggest that money frequently comes to you from unexpected sources. You could profit considerably from even a cursory study of bookkeeping and accounting.

If your total is EIGHT the acquisition of money appears to be second nature to you. You associate money with power, and with members of the opposite sex. Your subconscious reaction to money is indeed active. There is no halfway where you and money are concerned. It is either all the way or nothing at all. Your obvious lesson is one of BALANCE—the obtaining of a sense of balance. Otherwise you tend to have PLENTY OF NOTHING. Do not make the mistake of judging people by the size of their bank accounts. Money doesn't make a person either good or bad. At all times, it is the individual who counts, not how much or how little cash he has on deposit. In all, you appear assured of money—if intense interest in a subject has anything at all to do with acquisition.

If your total is NINE money seems to represent UNIVERSAL APPEAL. Your attitude is that "money makes the world go round." You may be right, too! But it takes more than money alone to make things happen: your subconscious number selection reveals that indeed you are very aware of this fact. However, money is also a matter of PRIDE to you. Having enough cash enables you to fulfill wishes, to help others, to "get around." As far as you are concerned, money is required in order to fully express your potential. Your sights are set high, your goal is universal. Your "costs" are secondary to your objective. With this kind of attitude, money is really secondary. The indications are that you will succeed!

If your total is ELEVEN you are likely to be most concerned with *how* you make your money. Money, in itself, might be secondary in importance. You tend (through your instantaneous number selection) to place more emphasis on the romantic, on devising sensational or unusual methods of acquiring capital. Money, for you, enhances you to *others*. This is significant. You, yourself, are not likely to feel any different, rich or poor. But you *project;* you wonder, for example, how Jill and Jim will feel once you have made your fortune. Or, on the opposite track, what they will think of you if you *fail* to become affluent. Recognize this tendency; deal with it, know it, master it. Live your own life, fulfill your *own* desires in money matters—be *less* concerned with what Jill or Jim will think. Basically, you are more likely to be happy through utilization of the occult or unusual or through progressive techniques in making your way in the material world.

If your total is TWENTY-TWO your subconscious attitude toward money is one that could lead you to success in the world of commerce. You are not afraid. This is the significant point: not afraid to tear down in order to rebuild, not afraid to admit an error in order to start over on the right path. Money does not awe you. You have a healthy respect for it, but you are the MASTER and money is the MEDIUM, which is a constructive subconscious reaction. You hurt yourself when you *limit ideas*. Allow yourself to be EXPANSIVE. Do not be concerned about expense. Needling or endless bickering can ruin chances for your success in money matters. Be practical as a BASIS FOR BUILDING. Be willing to TAKE LEAVE OF PRACTICALITY, as generally interpreted or understood by the majority, IN ORDER TO MAKE DREAMS TURN TO REALITIES.

17

Success

"Success"! It seems to be an American word, a peculiar American phenomenon—the drive for success, the striving for it, the thinking about it, the dreaming about it. Your dreams of success—the subconscious ones—often are buried deep, hidden from the conscious mind. But through our spontaneous number-selection technique, we are often able to probe deep, shaking hands with the truth that inhabits us all.

Let us try our method on YOU and your subconscious thoughts regarding SUCCESS.

Success, of course, is many things to many persons. And as each of us reaches maturity, success or the lack of it assumes added importance. What you *think* about success may well have much to do with whether or not you are able to attain it. And your ideas, or thoughts, about that elusive commodity are probably entirely different from the notions held by the next person.

First, relax. Then, think of SUCCESS. When you have that thought clearly formed in your mind, check any three of the numbers shown below:

1	2	3
4	5	6
7	8	9
	11 22	

Now, add your three numbers and reduce to a single total between 1 and 9. Simply add from left to right until you arrive at a single number. Retain only 11 or 22 as double totals.

For example, suppose you checked the numbers 1, 5 and 6. Your total, of course, would be 12 (1 plus 5 plus 6). Then you add the 12 total from left to right and arrive at a single digit, which would be 3 (1 plus 2). A very simple procedure, but most revealing, as you will see when you read what your number total indicates about you—and SUCCESS!

IF YOUR TOTAL IS 1, success, as far as you are concerned, means the blazing of new trails: it is being a pioneer, being independent, being able to make up your own mind and arrive at your own decisions. Your idea of success parallels some of the finest instincts of the founding fathers of this country. If you can live up to your subconscious concept of success—then there is little doubt you *will* be successful. Good luck!

IF YOUR TOTAL IS 2, some of the guys and gals might think your notions of success denote laziness. But this is not necessarily so! It's just that you are fond of relaxation; you feel that success means the right to go fishing, or listen to the hi-fi, or to do whatever your pleasure instincts dictate. Of course, carried to extremes, this subconscious notion could result in apathy. However, on the constructive side, your ideas about success could lead you into cultural fields, including the creative aspects of music and literature. Stick to your guns!

IF YOUR TOTAL IS 3, your spontaneous number selection reveals an attitude toward success best described as "too much"! Key words are "expansion," "fortune" and "beauty," as well as "luxury" and "money." In other words, you have an almost classic attitude toward success. In order to fulfill your dreams, however, you will have to avoid scattering your forces. Finish what you start instead of riding off in all directions at once.

IF YOUR TOTAL IS 4, success means hard work. Perhaps you have the most practical of all attitudes: you know there are obstacles to overcome and you appear quite willing to work your way up the ladder. You can go very far indeed if you understand that success usually involves perspiration. Persevere, but keep smiling.

IF YOUR TOTAL IS 5, success is associated with travel, excitement, creative activity—and romance. Your friends are right when they sometimes refer to you as an "incurable romantic." When you think of success, you are thinking of world-wide recognition. You may become a great detective or journalist. With you it is either all the way or nothing at all. Hasten to communicate your ideas. Qualifying yourself in this area means study, reading, appreciation of the arts and knowledge of current events.

IF YOUR TOTAL IS 6, success has much to do with a happy home life, with marriage, children and domestic tranquillity. In expressing this spontaneous number total, you reveal a mature attitude and lessen the odds toward your goal. What you desire is not the spectacular, but a steady stream of happiness and warmth based on love. Many of your friends tell you not to be so sentimental; pay them no heed. A home of your own will pay an increasingly important role in your life as you grow older. Success seems assured.

IF YOUR TOTAL IS 7 you are very idealistic in your concept of success. You dream of perfection, of complete inner and outer harmony. Your thoughts are concerned with marriage, with the perfect partner. This, of course, is not always easy to attain. But with this subconscious desire so strongly implanted your chances are good. It is often difficult for you to define what you actually mean by "success." But you are not the type of person to compromise. Whomever you choose as your life partner—the one who will eventually share your dreams, hopes and wishes—will indeed be a lucky individual.

IF YOUR TOTAL IS 8 there is no beating around the bush with you. Success is money. You think of success as the power, the ability to achieve your heart's desire. Often, this is tied up with the material things of life. But as you grow older and your best qualities develop, your ideas may well undergo gradual changes. Money is important, no one would deny that. But so are ideals and the self-satisfaction that comes with a job well done. You will have a better chance of achieving your startlingly high goals once materialism is mingled with a dose of altruism. You are to be admired for dreaming so ambitiously.

IF YOUR TOTAL IS 9 your idea of success is apt to feature international publicity and acclaim. Your ideas are big. There is nothing petty about your thinking, conscious or subconscious. With you it is all the way to the top. You can best achieve success through the creative arts or by cultivating a sense of *appreciation* for the efforts of others. You are an idealist; you are sympathetic; you are the natural humanitarian. It would be wise to bet on your chances. You are inclined TOWARD success.

IF YOUR TOTAL IS 11 your subconscious reaction to SUCCESS is marked by a *deviation from the norm*. You envision yourself choosing by-ways that others fear or are not aware of. You are a pioneer when it comes to succeeding. Once you begin to follow the worn and weary paths, you start to wane. This subconscious indicator does warn, however, against being different just for the sake of sensationalism or of attracting attention. You could become a lonely, unhappy person unless you are *thoroughly schooled* in your field of endeavor, which might well be television, aviation, astrology, ESP or work with techniques outlined here. Follow first impressions; your intuition should be of tremendous aid to you.

IF YOUR TOTAL IS 22 and you are young, your basic success attitudes are marked by maturity. Deep within you tend to associate success with personal magnetism, with persuasiveness, with a winning personality. You recognize values of SALESMANSHIP. This will stand you in good stead, UNLESS YOU SWING TOWARD OUT-AND-OUT COMMERCIALISM. Your attitudes (subconscious indicator) are attractive only insofar as they promote a FASCINATING UNIQUENESS of approach. Avoid the heavy hand. Tell your story, but sell yourself with a SUBTLE touch. Otherwise you will be laughed at instead of listened to. Remember that nothing is likely to be permanent except CHANGE (which means that you should be willing to retrace your steps or reconsider original ideas in order to arrive at your greatest potential).

18

The People You Attract

This test attempts to tell you something about the man or woman you attract. And the results should also give you some pertinent information about yourself as well as persons who are attracted to you.

Simply relax and think of or visualize your ideal man or woman, as the case may be. Then check any three numbers below:

1	3	5	7	11	22
2	4	6	8	9	

Add the total of your number selections and reduce to a single digit between 1 and 9. The only double numbers retained as final totals are 11 and 22.

TOTALS:

ONE—Those members of the opposite sex who are attracted to you are NOT apt to be shrinking violets. Instead they tend to be forceful, dominant, original, independent. They may aspire to the theater, the world of entertainment. Those attracted to you have sex appeal, are able to project their personalities—and may very well be temperamental to an extreme!

TWO—You seem to attract true romantics. Mostly, they are steadfast, loyal and have an eye to the future—as well as stars in their eyes. You are warned, however, that frivolous action—on your part—could disillusion them and finally drive them away. You tend to attract those who have an apreciation of home life and home cooking.

You attract (and are attracted to) persons who have their eyes pointed toward the heavens and their feet firmly on the ground.

THREE—Members of the opposite sex who are intrigued by you are very likely to be those who love parties, who are happiest when the subject matter is light, and who have boundless energy. You may, at times, have trouble keeping up with your admirers. They are apt to be considered lucky because they generally appear to be HAPPY. Those who are drawn to you are persons who like to travel, who have respect for education, but who skip over their studies and thus attain only superficial knowledge. Others may tend to be jealous of your good fortune in attracting such lively individuals. Be wary, however, or you may find yourself completely scattering your forces.

FOUR—Those of the opposite sex who are attracted to you are apt to be solid, steady and strong. Such people are great admirers of the truth. You can get along with them by being forthright, honest, by speaking from the heart. If anyone can tag a phony, the people you attract certainly can. You are lucky. Those attracted to you are not out to fool you.

FIVE—You attract persons who abound in sex appeal. Those who really dig you are filled with life, creative forces, are likely to be artists, writers, entertainers, or follow a line of endeavor that emphasizes self-expression. You must be quite a person yourself to attract these members of the opposite sex! To have continued social success, keep up with the world. Read and pursue a creative hobby. Otherwise you will be by-passed.

SIX—Those of the opposite sex who are drawn to you are lovers of luxury, the finer things of life, including good music and books. You attract truly mature people. No child's play here, which means you have a challenge. You too must be grown-up, must have adult tastes. You are to be complimented. Those you attract appear to have a great sense of discrimination.

SEVEN—Members of the opposite sex, interested in you, are generally moody, independent to the nth degree, and very serious indeed. It is very often up to you to inject some humor into a social situation. You attract people who are concerned with abstract principles. They know the meanings of words like "integrity" and "honesty" and "sincerity." And they often quote poetry.

EIGHT—Persons attracted to you are business leaders of the future. They are immensely capable people who are blessed with charisma. These people have a sense of responsibility. They are not afraid of hard work. They like money but are not fanatical on the subject. But just don't try to borrow without offering collateral. You are to be congratulated. You attract members of the opposite sex who will be very popular and successful.

NINE—You interest members of the opposite sex who are truly idealists. So you must be distinctly individual yourself. The people who lean toward you are fiery in their beliefs. They will not compromise on principles. They are very sympathetic and will always side with the underdog. One of them could become world famous. To keep up with the people you attract, you must make yourself familiar with art, music and literature.

ELEVEN—You fascinate persons whose interests border on the unusual: astrology, graphology, palmistry, numerology, modern art, underground elements in modern literature, etc. The man or woman drawn to you (and by the same token—the *kind* of man or woman you *desire* to attract) is a SEARCHER, a SEEKER, one who is never satisfied with the status quo—one who believes in TRUTH as AUTHORITY—one who feels truth is not always to be found in textbooks. These men or women are certainly out-of-the-ordinary and they will instruct and entertain you. Never turn away when they need help. If you neglect such friends, you are going against your basic desires.

TWENTY-TWO—Your subconscious indicator here points to attraction of men or women who are creative, idealistic, and who can teach the world many vital truths. Because you attract this type of individual, you are basically an exciting, challenging person, who may eventually be associated with the communications field, publishing, radio, television, etc. Your key word is CREATE. Once you become smug or permanently satisfied with things as they are, you are on the road toward loss of friends—and loss of a vital part of yourself.

Part THREE

19

Thought Dial as Time Machine

If the subconscious, through Thought Dial, can express a numerical symbol that can be analyzed and acted upon, the procedure can also be reversed. The subconscious lacks a sense of humor. The signals you offer it are often returned to you in starkly literal form. Be specific. Don't ask frivolous questions.

If, through the Thought Dial technique, your subconscious comes up, let us say, with a total of six, we know that you are concerned with such things as home, domestic adjustment or a vexing family situation. Conversely, if you consciously feel the need of a new house, a domestic adjustment, renewed family ties, greater understanding of family members, try to *feel* the home, the adjustment, the change, the harmonious familial relationship—and TURN THE DIAL TO NUMBER 6.

When this occurs, you *feed the subconscious a concept*, a plan, image, thought, idea, or desire. Leave the dial on the number you desire. By way of experimenting, try placing the dial on 1. In a matter of days, if not hours, you will enjoy new contacts, greater opportunity for creative experiment, calls from people who would like to know you. There will be challenges which, if met, will lead to greater independence of thought and action. Clearly, then, we are *directing* instead of accepting directions from the subconscious by this reverse procedure.

Why should this be? Why does it work? I can only theorize. I suppose that once we dial to the selected Thought Dial number we are planting the seed of an idea that the subconscious nourishes until the abstract is transformed into the concrete. A revolutionary concept? Perhaps. But I strongly suspect that this is an ancient technique, an instinctive and universal truth. It really does not matter *how* this technique works. What does matter is that it is effective.

It is necessary to familiarize ourselves yet again with the basic meanings of the numbers. These meanings have been handed down traditionally, have been discovered through research and experimentation. Specifically, in working these many years with the Thought Dial concept, I have learned what the numbers symbolize. Your own experiments, I am sure, will add dimension to the findings set forth here. Our understanding of the numbers and their meanings grow as we work with them, as we prod, test, probe and find ourselves either right or wrong in attempting to locate lost articles, pick winners, tap the subconscious and answer direct questions. Now we have arrived at the "reversal point," the point of feeding information to the subconscious—the point of directing and controlling our fate. To do this we must know, with the familiarity that grows out of certainty, what we are asking—and this makes it necessary to know the numbers.

We must know what we are asking. We must know what we are directing, what we are requesting, what we want to bring about, what we want to make occur. We must, in other words, know what we are putting into that computer which is, for our purpose, the subconscious. Thus, if I set the Thought Dial on 1, I must know what it is that 1 represents—and the same applies, of course, in connection with the other numbers.

Setting Your Time

As I write I want ideas to flow from my brain to paper; I want to communicate my thoughts to you. Thus I have set my Thought Dial on number 5. It has been on this digit for a few days, accumulating strength, gathering ammunition, building up force. Now I am releasing it.

Why is the dial set on 5? Number 5 is Mercury, the planetary symbol of thought process; Mercury is associated with the Third House, having to do with ideas, writing. Number 5 is Mercury, the Winged Messenger, and signifies change, variety, communication of thoughts, personal magnetism, activity connected with putting ideas on paper.

For publishing itself, we could place the dial on 3, which is related to long-range planning. But 3 tends to lead to a scattering of forces, is experimentation—the give-and-take of discussion relating, among other things, to publishing projects. Number 3 is also socializing, the invigoration that contact with people brings about. It is more the preparation and publication of a book than the actual writing of it. Number 5, on the other hand, is the actual putting of words to paper. And that is why, at the present time, my personal Thought Dial rests on number 5.

Of course we have provided a superficial example, but the idea is specific, simple. This new area, this time-machine concept, is not different. It is merely reversed—from pouring out to pouring in to the subconscious. WE ARE DIALING THE KIND OF TIME WE DESIRE.

Before deciding upon a specific "time" or number, it is advisable to permit the dial to rest on zero. That is our starting point. It is neutral.

Now, what do we want? Well, on a superficial level, the answer is not difficult to discern. A new start is 1, commercial activity is 8, love and sex could be 8 or 5, while the completion of a project would naturally be 9. Increased social activity would be 3, while a change of residence or domestic adjustment would be 6. An inward look, greater self-analysis, would be 7, while an ability to wait, to absorb knowledge would be 2—attention to details would dictate number 4. Interest in the occult, in teaching, would bring us to 11, while a tearing down in order to rebuild would take us to the other double number, 22.

But how do we discover, on a deeper level, what it is we need, what number we want to feed to the subconscious? Perhaps writer Henry Miller's comment can help in this direction. The famed literary figure states, "The value of the Thought Dial lies in the discovery—sooner or later—that all the answers to all questions must come from within. When one becomes truly aware of this an-cient truth one will learn to ask the right questions. The first thing to find out is—*who*—is asking *what*? Second, are you prepared to accept the response provoked?"

Well, if the questions come from within—as do the answers—so, too, must our knowledge of what we need to ask. Or, more properly, what we want to ask for, what "time" it is on which we wish to set our dial.

With this much on the record, let me suggest a prelimi-nary procedure. Turn first to the section on tapping the subconscious. Bring forth three numbers, with or without the actual Thought Dial. Add the numbers and reduce to a single digit between 1 and 9, with the exceptions of 11 and 22.

STUDY THE MESSAGE PROVIDED IN THE SECTION OF TAP-PING THE SUBCONSCIOUS. Reflect upon it. The idea is to find out in which direction you are going, to discover the "time" you want to create. Or, rather, the kind of time-climate you desire your subconscious to nourish and thus to transform to a reality.

That is one preliminary procedure. Another would be to place on paper a number of statements or aspirations in order to find out what you are missing. Where are you headed? Where do you want to go? Answer these and other questions in WRITING. Get your goal in sight. Is it a love affair that concerns you? IMAGE the person in ques-tion—see, hear, feel the individual in your mind's eye. Concentrate on an understanding, a visualization of what you want to attract, accomplish, bring to pass, material-ize. And another point: DO NOT BE CONCERNED WITH HOW THIS "TIME" WILL COME TO BE A REALITY. *That is the job of the subconscious!* It is a task the subconscious is eminently qualified for. It gets the job done, brings about the time you desire. And your desire is indicated by the *time* on which you set your Thought Dial.

A woman who was troubled with noisy neighbors, a rambunctious daughter, lack of peace and harmony, turned the dial to 6. In her words: "All of a sudden, or so it seemed, everything became tranquil. My daughter, who has been argumentative and lonely, found a wonderful man and got married. The house seems quieter now. I have moved into her bedroom, which seems to be noise-free. I am taking greater interest in the beautification of my apartment now that my daughter and her husband have taken our pet cat to live with them. I enjoy my apartment more than ever since undertaking this experiment with Thought Dial, since turning it to number 6, as suggested."

The above is a simple example. The woman in question did not ask for the impossible, although peace and quiet, at the time, seemed far away, almost divorced from reality. You might say this was a coincidence. And indeed it was. It was a *coinciding* of Thought Dial set on 6 and events changing in the home. Such coincidences make up a fact and cause us to believe that Thought Dial, for whatever hidden or obscure reason, does work.

The task is to find out what time we want and then to set it. I have offered some suggestions for preliminary procedure. Now I am going to tell you as much as I can about the numbers, the symbols—information gleaned through experience—and I want you to study these number descriptions. Then, as in the chapter "Picking Winners," decide for yourself what is meaningful to you. Number 1, for example, might fill the bill for a certain individual, since it features new starts and added independence. For another person, number 1 might be the answer, but for an entirely different reason. Number 1 could be the new start, but it could also represent greater creative satisfaction, better relations with children and a new love affair.

Obviously, the symbols, the numbers, are many-sided. You must, therefore, outline your needs, tap your subconscious. You must form an image of what you require, want, desire, need; then, study the information we are about to provide. If your own inner vision is clear, there will be a *spark of recognition* when you come across the right number or symbol for your requirements. When this has been accomplished, deliberately set your dial (time) and place the TD on a bookcase, table, a prominent yet not overly conspicuous spot. If you feel the need, carry your Thought Dial with you when you go out; or leave one, with your "time" set, in your home. Carry another, with the appropriate setting, with you.

Thus you will have dialed or set your psychological time

and your subconscious will get busy doing the rest—if you so permit it.

Number One Time

Here we are involved with a time of greater individuality, a need to be selfish about our needs. You get, during this time, the drive, the ability to bring about a change, to shake off the old and to begin building for the future. YOUR APPEARANCE UNDERGOES A CHANGE. THE OLD YOU IS GONE—THERE CAN BE A RENEWED VITALITY, VIGOR, WHICH CAUSES MANY TO THINK ABOUT AND COMMENT ON THE "NEW YOU."

This is a time when your individuality shines forth, when your personal-magnetism rating is high. It is a time that attracts the opposite sex. It could be a time when a relationship grows into a meaningful alliance, such as marriage. It is the planting of a seed that could develop in marriage, family. It is a time when you must take the INITIAL STEP. The step is a form of speculation; it makes you independent of the crowd.

This is a time in which you invent, promote original ideas. There is a creative force evident that makes it necessary for you to seek greater self-expression. This could come in the form of physical love, writing, painting, teaching children. It is a time not only of independence, but of a certain amount of aggression; time to take the lead, to march forward, to invent new procedures for home and office. A time is shown for wearing distinctive clothes, for being daring in dress and manner. Obviously, this is a time for action. It is a building period, a time to move ahead and, perhaps, to leave relics behind.

On a short-range basis, it is a time to sell yourself and your ideas, to make contacts, get in to see the top man. On a long-range basis, the dial set on number 1 brings about psychological changes that will help you overcome shyness and make you appear selfish, but will actually work toward greater determination, conviction, adherence to principles.

Long or short range, this is an active period. Number 1, as pointed out earlier, is the Sun, and its light shines on you. If it is the spotlight you desire, you've dialed the right number. But if it is solitude you need, then you have the wrong symbol.

Dialing number 1 is apt to bring you in contact with individuals born under Leo, from July 23 to August 22. Feeding number 1 to your subconscious precipitates an active period; you are dialing a time that can be filled with changes, can force an attitude of greater independence. It is excellent where INVENTIONS are concerned. It also promotes better physical relations with the opposite sex and tends to create children.

As indicated in the section "Tapping the Subconscious," the creative urge is strong. The need is not only for sex expression but for new forms of expression, for an original way of presenting an old package. This is the numerical symbol to be utilized when presenting a format, for breaking from the old, for discarding the hackneyed.

This is the number (time) for taking a chance, for getting in on the ground floor, for beginning an enterprise, promoting yourself. It is a time to blow your own horn, to let others know not only that you exist but that you have an imprint of your own, an individual personality and a unique style.

Expect new contacts. Be ready for romance. Take a chance. Give up the old in favor of new opportunity. Dialing to number 1 draws attention, causes others to be attracted, pushes personal magnetism to the degree that you sell, persuade, are dynamic and desirable to the opposite sex.

Don't expect the status quo; the old labels vanish. New duties crop up, along with challenges. This is the time for pioneering action.

Develop power of will. This is necessary because you have dialed a time of challenge. Do things creatively; don't follow the crowd. Now, if this advice is followed, you are going to alienate some persons. You will be regarded as a challenge or threat, an individual who wants to upset old ways, to bring about reforms. Some may try to circulate rumors about you, term you as radical. Others, a minority, will be attracted and will defend you. In any case, you will attract controversy. If you are not prepared to accept these changes, *Don't* dial 1. However, if indeed you are ready for a new deal, for greater personal satisfaction, then you are on the right "time line."

If you weaken, you will find that others boss you. If you are not strong in convictions, others will push you, attempting to keep you at the bottom instead of giving you a chance to rise to the top. It is up to you to stand up for your convictions, to exhibit the courage necessary for leading rather than following. Number 1 makes demands, and unless you are ready for a struggle, get off this wave length.

The key here is affirmation, self-reliance, a throwing off of dependence on others. You begin the climb, perhaps alone. But there is movement, there is change and challenge; and, most important, there is an attraction to opportunity, creativity, love, sex, brightness rather than the darkness of being alone. In a sense you are alone in principles, beliefs, faith in the new, in a creative process. But the light of inspiration is bright, bright enough to attract others. Not all agree, but the controversy can be transformed into something constructive. Number 1 is forceful, dominant. In so dialing, you are asking for a chance, a change; you are drawing love and with it you must also accept added pressure and responsibility.

Does this strike a responsive chord? If so, number 1 is the time you need. If not, forego number 1, for it is not yet your time. Number 1 makes you an individual of distinction. Certainly some persons will point an accusing finger. Others will point in a friendly, admiring way, holding you up as an example, a pioneer, one who displayed the gumption to hurdle barriers, throw off jealousies; one who was determined to climb and did so. Number 1 is not going to leave you alone. It is a persistent time; the challenge is ever present and demands that you be selfish enough to get the necessary material, to obtain the required backing, to take the key steps.

You needn't grit your teeth or clench your fists; you need not force issues. The subconscious will take over and you will be progressing along pioneer trails.

Are you afraid to tackle the new? If the answer is YES, skip number 1.

Are you intrigued by adventure, challenge, romance, a new start? If the answer is YES, this is your time, your number. Feed it to the subconscious by dialing number 1 on your Thought Dial.

This is a cycle of seeking, of finding, of sighting a goal and then moving toward it. It is not a number of procrastination. Leave the philosophizing for another time. Leave the doubts, even reasoning, for another time. THIS TIME IS FOR DIRECT, EVEN SELFISH, ACTION. If you are dialing number 1, you've had enough of others' woes, you are ready for new, unique experiences. You have determined that the old regime, the old habit patterns, are to be broken. You must be ready for direct confrontation. Furthermore, it must be you who blazes the trail, who fires up the creative urge. IF YOU SET THAT DIAL ON 1 YOU ARE GOING TO WANT TO CREATE—to write, paint, sing, carve, sculpt. You are going to give of yourself and demand payment, recognition, without being shy about setting your price.

If you are to respond to the positive side of this time, this number 1 subconscious symbol, then you will favor progress. You will be confident without braggadocio. You will be determined without being stubborn. You will shake off fear of the unknown, avoid stagnation, be dominant without being a bully. You will state your case without inviting antagonism.

In determining that the number 1 time is to be your time, you handle major issues and leave the minor ones to others. In deciding on this time, you cultivate new contacts and create a broader base of interests.

You ACCOMPLISH because you can create something out of nothing. You plant the seeds. You give birth to opportunity.

Number 1 is the Fifth House and, thus, there is love, sex and activity connected with children. There is the providing of entertainment, the basking in the spotlight. There is a willingness to leave one's self open to criticism as well as praise.

Setting your Thought Dial on 1 could make you an originator, a promoter; your subconscious is directed to capture new fields, to conquer new heights. You, through placing the dial on number 1, are asking to be the leader. YOU ARE ENTERPRISING, DARING, DYNAMIC, READY TO LEAD THE WAY AND TO DIRECT OTHERS IN SALESMANSHIP, PROMOTION AND NEW CONCEPTS IN ADVERTISING. YOU ARE THE PRODUCER OF THE FORMAT THAT OUTDOES THOSE NOW IN EXISTENCE.

Are you ready? Did you get a flash of recognition when

reading number 1 under "Your Subconscious Thoughts"? If so, then set your dial on 1. You'll get what you ask for. Just remember that you did ask for it.

By dialing number 1, you "tune in" on the ability to advance your own interest among persons of influence. You put yourself in a position to make contact with those who have power, who can grant privileges. You are dialing a time when solicitation can be made for special opportunities and concessions, such as employment, benefits, loans, releases, even favors in the form of unusual postponements.

If you want to push yourself forward, and if you're not afraid of the bright light of attention, this is your time.

Number Two Time

When you dial number 2, you are asking for a time to absorb, to catch up following a period of frenzied activity. Study the number 2 section of "Your Subconscious Thoughts." You will find that this represents a need for diplomacy, whereby you can win your way rather than force issues.

When you feed the 2 symbol to your subconscious, you are delaying, or avoiding abrupt decisions. Number 2 is associated with the Moon and brings you in contact with persons born under the zodiacal sign of *Cancer,* from June 21 to July 22.

This is a time when you COLLECT, WHEN YOU HATCH THE PROVERBIAL NEST EGG. It is a time to save time, money, and energy, psychic and physical.

If your pace has been too quick, if life has been hectic, if you have been on a dizzying merry-go-round, then, indeed, your time should now be number 2.

If you have recently been caught in a triangle, you need the respite offered by the number 2 time. If you place your Thought Dial on 2, the subconscious is being computerized to work out questions, problems concerning security, home, one of your parents. You are dialing a time when you collect debts, a time when you accumulate saving. To do this, be ready to forego pleasures, extravagances; you can't spend and save at the same time.

This is a symbol of gaining, but also of getting rid of surplus. Be frugal without being miserly. Know your limitations without losing your confidence.

You have dialed a time of watchful waiting. You should dial 2 if you are seeking property, looking for a home, planning on building, improving your security.

Don't dial 2 if you are impatient for results. Dial this symbol if you are willing to build on a solid base, to discard the superficial, to cement family relations.

This is a time when you PREPARE: facts, formats, plans, blueprints, for the future; when you work out a budget, and adhere to it. You dial 2 when, after having initiated a project, you must build good will. You enhance the value of a project, of property, during this time. We all, of course, require such opportunities. And if you have struck a chord of recognition here, this is your time, a time to build, to gain *psychic income*. During such times it is, very often, difficult to put your finger on *exact* values. This is because of the duality of number 2.

THIS IS THE TIME TO COMPLETE FACTS, INFORMATION. You round out, mature, survey, perceive. You *feel* rather than act. The Moon is emotional and subject to change. During this time you can observe the way the wind blows, you can watch the scales swing back and forth, you can pinpoint your best move through keen observation.

If you dial number 2, you have recently made some abrasive contacts. Now you can build fences. You can smooth over the rough edges. That's the kind of cycle (time) you have dialed.

AVOID being overcritical, impatient. Don't brood, worry or nag. ACCEPT rather than reject. By this is meant develop a *spirit of acceptance*. Be analytical without being immobile. Be patient without being frozen. Seek security without being married to tradition. It is a time when you contemplate marriage (if single), or a new or more complete home (if married). An addition to the family, or greater family responsibility, also coincides with this time.

With no control (negative) you are drawn in several directions: here and there, up and down, forward and backward (Cancer zodiacal sign). With control you are capable, finally, of deciding—making decisions based on accumulated knowledge.

Now, a key point with this time is that you may tend to get so wrapped up in facts, figures, statistics and details that you neglect your appearance, and your social contacts. Avoid this tendency. To use a cliché, all work and no play will certainly add up to a dull score. After all, in dialing this time, you should be seeking improved family relations, a better environment at the home base. In *seeking* do not fail to see the trees for the forest. Do not alienate the very persons (close ties, family members) for whom you seek to provide greater stability.

Be impressionable without believing everything you read, hear or see. Don't be naive enough to fall prey to every impression, mood, report or rumor. Realize that statistics can be deceiving. Gather, collect, save, file—but always, always be on the lookout for the nonessential, the debris, the junk. Don't be afraid to throw away as well as collect.

If you become a victim of constant vacillation, you will also be a tool of those who want to dominate rather than guide.

You seek, when placing your Thought Dial on 2, to gain protection; you hunger for warmth, love, affection. You want to embrace security. In so dialing, you will gain a valuable ally in your subconscious. BUT, you can also surround yourself with more than you bargained for. You will have to be unobtrusive, to make headway slowly. If you are not on the alert, you will be prodding rather than wise, dense rather than perceptive.

On the constructive side, you can minister to the needs of your family. You can build a base upon which love flourishes.

AN OLDER WOMAN could enter the picture during this time period, and significant decisions could center about this individual, whether she be mother, aunt, or advisor.

During this period, it is essential to watch your weight. Be aware of diet and general appearance; don't get run down at the heels. You are busy where the large projects are concerned, such as moving your home, planning a voyage.

Dial 2 for business dealing with movable things, projects of indefinite location. You work, during this time cycle, with chemicals, with staples, such as milk, gasoline and other liquids.

YOU DO NOT BEGIN OR START OR INITIATE: you've already done that and now you are absorbing information in preparation for expansion. This is not a permanent period.

BUT YOU DO MAKE THE PLANS THAT LEAD TO GREATER STABILITY. That's the kind of time you have dialed.

In dialing 2, you invite a period of rehabilitation. You feed to your subconscious an order to re-evaluate, to collect and select.

This symbol seems to attract to you persons who deal in real estate and with persons who could advise you on the future. These people are capable of making money for you, especially if you were born under Gemini, from May 21 to June 20. And, if you were born under restless Gemini, the need for this numerical (2) symbol is necessary from time to time, as it is for all of us.

By slowing down, which this dial setting encourages, you give yourself a chance to catch up. You see, you are not standing still, but merely changing your pace. And a change of pace can be beneficial, as you will see.

During this period you learn to avoid excess. You recoup, collect, earn and save. This is in contrast to other times, when you spend, speculate and gamble. During this period you neither borrow or lend; you measure, discover your capabilities and your own pace.

Dialing 2 coincides with a time when you are a homemaker. You work harmoniously with others; you repair damage to the house and, more importantly, you heal wounds inflicted on family members.

Number 2 is a conservative time, but it is not fixed. That is, you are merely drawing a breath, recuperating, getting ready, preparing for the future. Know this and don't become mired down with nonessentials. DON'T BE POSSESSED BY POSSESSIONS. Be comfortable without cluttering your life with this, that and everything you can grab. GET WHAT YOU NEED. Anything extra is going to be discarded, so don't waste time and money piling up material goods. And avoid a maudlin attitude. If not wary during this period you can become too soft.

Dialing number 2 is tuning in on a time when you attract and absorb many things. You become interested, fascinated with food, home, perhaps the stock market. There is a possibility that you will become engrossed in a hobby which, in the near future, is responsible for greater contacts, increased social activity and travel. You lay the ground work during this number 2 time.

This is a time when you are sensitive enough to be easily hurt. EMOTIONS ARE EXPOSED, RAW, INVITING SOME

TO TAKE ADVANTAGE OF YOU. If your guard is down you can fall in love with the wrong person.

Your own punches are pulled; you fear hurting others, but you leave yourself open to abuse. These are the negative aspects of the number 2 time.

Now, what is it you want? What you desire during this time is to love and be loved. You want the pace slowed so you can enjoy food, rest, recreation. You want to be surrounded by family, other loved ones. You want to heal emotional wounds. You want to settle down in an atmosphere of peace and harmony. If these things strike that chord of recognition, set your Thought Dial on 2.

With your dial on 2, you do the little things; the big things will take care of themselves. You build, especially with relation to home and property. You remain open-minded, welcoming ideas that stimulate.

This is basically a slow time, a time when you will be tempted to lose patience. As you mature, however, you will learn to pull in the reins, to pace yourself so there is something left for the end of the race. You are diplomatic, you collect facts, you face situations as they actually exist.

This period is climaxed by a greater degree of recognition; you receive publicity. You gain through women. You fulfill basic commitments. You receive an offer which makes it possible to either sell or buy a home. You find out where it is you are going—and why.

Number Three Time

This is a social time. You dial number 3 when you want to break out of a rut, emotional and otherwise. You dial this numerical symbol when you desire expansion, travel, the growth of a seed planted approximately two years earlier. This can also be a time of confusion, of not knowing whether to go or stay. Ideas and opportunities are plentiful. Be discriminating, choose the best, and the "best" is not necessarily the easiest course, the brightest-appearing or the most fun. It is necessary, in choosing this time, to accent quality over quantity. Number 3 time is related to Jupiter, the planet that rules Sagittarius and the

Ninth House. Thus, long journeys are involved; basic philosophy enters the picture, as does writing, being published, long-range projects. This is what can occur if you do not fall victim to helpless confusion.

Dialing number 3 is apt to bring you in contact with persons born under Sagittarius, from November 22 to December 21. Dialing this number "orders" your subconscious to attract a flurry of activity. YOU LIFT YOURSELF FROM AN EMOTIONAL MORASS. YOU GO PLACES, DO THINGS, ATTEND PARTIES, PARTICIPATE IN SOCIAL AFFAIRS.

If you're tired of a merry-go-round type of existence, DON'T dial 3. If you want to settle down rather than be on the move, AVOID this numerical symbol.

Number 3 is flexible, versatile, light-hearted. That's the atmosphere of time you are dialing when the Thought Dial is placed on 3.

With this number you are encountering what might be termed a "double-edged sword." I have found that, although 3 is activity and movement, it is also confusion and uncertainty. There is a contradiction, at least it so seems, in that you must settle down in order to accomplish anything. Yet 3 appears to be the opposite.

IF YOU ARE IN A STATE OF PANIC—ENERGY BEING SAPPED AND NOT KNOWING WHERE TO STOP—THIS IS YOUR NUMBER. Dialing 3 helps avoid panic (which must be avoided), because it brings to you an essential, invaluable element—the element of humor. You see the funny, even the ludicrous, side of events and situations.

IF YOU DON'T KNOW JUST WHAT IT IS YOU DESIRE you're tuned in to the right time. Number 3 is just that: an experiment, a casting about in an effort to gain solid footing.

Your intellectual curiosity is spurred by this time cycle. You find yourself in a position where you probe, travel, examine and investigate. But, on the negative side, you simply try too much at once. You scatter your forces. You spread yourself too thin.

DURING THIS TIME THERE IS A TENDENCY TO TRY MORE THAN YOU CAN HANDLE. The keynote of 3 is expansion and, if not careful, you could "expand" in a physical sense.

During this time there is less mental pressure than during other cycles, periods, time sequences. Thus, if you require concentration, avoid number 3. But if you want to lift mental burdens, dial number 3. If you want to accelerate your social obligations, avoid number 3. The choice is simple *if you will but examine your own motives.*

In dialing 3, be ready to tackle one thing at a time. Don't have too many irons in the fire.

You gain, through this time period, greater appreciation of what you possess. As we discovered in the chapter on "Your Subconscious Thoughts," this time period symbolizes joy in living, tells of improved social life, important contacts to be made at parties, gatherings and conferences.

IF YOU WANT TO PUBLISH, TRAVEL, PUT ACROSS A BASIC PHILOSOPHY, this is your number and your time.

You could overspend because of a light attitude toward responsibilities. Number 3, although a symbol of play, is nothing to play around with—not if you don't want to wake up empty-handed.

NUMBER 3 TIME ATTRACTS GREATER GENEROSITY. People tend to be more lenient with you during this time. Your errors are overlooked because some find it difficult to take you seriously. You deal more with thoughts, the abstract, than you do with tangibles. You can write and publish and project long-range plans. But, as for gaining immediate results, you are bucking the odds. So, as we stated, the 3 time is a two-sided coin. People are generous, forgive you and your mistakes, but, on the other hand, they don't tend to take seriously, your claims or efforts. That's the kind of time it is: light, devoid of great pressure; social, but, also lacking in a solid place to land, build, construct.

If you want to lift burdens, dial 3. But, remember, you are also dialing a time when people regard you as more of a lightweight than a person of substance. If you've been under pressure—all work, all concentration—then dial 3 for relief. It is a time for contacts, reaching out, looking ahead, and not a time for business as usual or attention to routine detail.

This is not the time to be tied down, either in business ventures or in personal life. YOU TEND, DURING THIS TIME, TO LOSE THINGS WHILE IN TRANSIT. YOU TEND TO BE OUT-OF-DOORS OR ON THE HIGH SEAS. Obviously, then, you only dial 3 when you want a change of pace, a change of scene.

DO YOU WANT CHEER, OPTIMISM? Then dial 3.

DO YOU WANT TO BE AWARE OF DETAILS AND KNOWL-
EDGABLE ABOUT FINE PRINT? Then avoid number 3.

In dialing this time your situation undergoes a change.
The walls of responsibility come tumbling down. You give
and receive invitations. Some of your social obligations
require travel and cost money. There is a whirlwind of
activity, none of it amounting to anything too solid. Is this
what you need, desire? Does this strike a chord of recognition, of need, a filling of emotional hunger? If so, dial
this time.

Artistic expression comes to the forefront here. You
share discoveries, pleasures and joys. People want to have
you around. They want to party with you, vacation with
you, do almost everything but work with you. Knowing
this, realizing that you are dialing a vacation from the
status quo more than anything else, act accordingly.

IF YOU DIAL 3 remember that your energies may be
scattered, so be sure to finish one thing before starting
another. Be joyful, but don't be a slave to frivolity. You
are, in dialing 3, tuning into a so-called higher mind
element. There is nothing petty about this period. You
will be dealing with concrete issues. You may not be
aware of all the details, but you will be concerned with
the overall ISSUES. Morality and its long-range implications play a role here. The question of whether the ends
justify the means enters the picture. You may think that
dialing 3 is all fun and games. But 3 brings with it a
philosophical responsibility, a moral one, a time for
finding out how far you want to go, how much you want
to extend yourself. Number 3 does bring fun, but only in
contrast to trouble; it brings light only in contrast to
previous darkness. Number 3, dialed only to evade responsibility, can bring more problems than you might imagine.

During this time, seek, look, check, investigate. The
element of timing or luck enters. Social activities are
going to be increased. You are not going to sit by that
fireplace and meditate; instead, with 3 on your dial, you're
going to be on the move. You are going to make contact
with those who are intrigued with you. They will want to
hear your ideas. A sense of humor, as already stated, will
be necessary. You will be so active that the tendency will
be to overlook details. Mistakes will result. Your image
will be that of a happy-go-lucky person who is absent-
minded, perhaps highly creative, but one who does not

necessarily keep appointments or accurate records. Only charm and humor can balance the scales in your favor during this typical 3 period.

If you dial 3, be ready to hand over the details to others. You take the long-range view but leave the accounting, the bookkeeping, to associates, friends, co-workers. Your head for figures is apt to be fuzzy. During this time, far-ranging communication lines are set up. You are given opportunities; someone at a distance could play a significant role. The subconscious here aims at expansion, greater income and increased social activity. Number 3 time points to the outdoors and to Sagittarius, which is associated with the hips and thighs. Know this and be wary lest injury occurs to those parts of the body.

Your impulse here is to accomplish great things; you want to reform the world, to right the wrongs of your own environment and to reach out and spread good will. Taken literally, these impulses could lead you to an emotional punch in the nose. Your fervor is intense during this time. BUT IT IS NOT LIKELY TO BE TAKEN SERIOUSLY BY OTHERS. Know this and don't permit yourself to develop a neurosis. When you dial 3, as we say, it's not all beer and skittles. After the party there is a reckoning. And, for you, it is likely to be the same as it is for almost anyone with a heavy hangover: a time to swear off, to reform, to be utra-serious. DON'T DIAL 3 WITH THE EXPECTATION OF CHANGING THE WORLD. DIAL 3 IF YOU WANT TO LUXURIATE IN AN ATMOSPHERE OF VANISHING CARES, OF PARTIES PRODUCING PLEASING EFFECTS, OF SOCIAL CONTACTS that—*in the future*—MAY BEAR FRUIT.

You are dialing, in 3, a time when the light touch is your identity no matter how heavy-handed you may want to appear. Unless you realize this, you are inviting grief.

Ask yourself why you want 3. Perhaps it is a respite from loneliness, a relief of routine without forever abandoning responsibility. I would feel you want time to get your thoughts on paper without feeling too intense about it.

BUT I WOULD NOT WANT YOU TO DIAL 3 FOR MERE ESCAPISM. *It simply doesn't work that way.*

Number Four Time

When dialing 4 you are attracting settled conditions where discipline and routine prevail; but you also desire to break away. This is contradictory on the surface, but it amounts to a need to LEARN THE RULES BEFORE YOU BREAK THEM.

If you've been at loose ends lately, this is the time cycle for you. If you want to be aware of the fine print, shrewd enough to read between the lines, yet creative enough to know that barriers can be broken and experience enhanced, then the 4 time should be your time.

Now, during the 4 period, is the time to check routine, catch up on details, NOT the time to escape, to fly off in numerous directions at once.

During this period you attract persons born under Aquarius, from January 20 to February 18, and under the zodiacal sign of Leo, from July 23 to August 22.

Now is the time to attend to basic tasks in person. Don't trust details to others; don't delegate too many duties. Your patience will be tired, but this is a necessary period of self-discipline. If you are weary of trying to be everywhere at once, weary of chasing a rainbow, tired of promises that have no solid base, dial number 4. In so doing your work is cut out for you, but you will have something to show for it.

This is the time when an obstacle can be overcome, when those opposing you can be transformed into enthusiastic allies. This is a time when success depends upon your willingness to see a project through to completion. You have to wait, but the wait proves worthwhile.

You place your Thought Dial on 4 when you grow weary of unimportant activity and are ready to get down to essentials, when you desire a "testing time." You work, wait, test, accomplish, placing one stone upon another until a building is constructed.

This time symbol attracts to you solid citizens with solid propositions. It repels those who are merely out for a good time. If the good times, the social life, have worn your nerves and have caused you to become impatient with tea parties and the "nice" approach—then set that dial on 4. In turn you will attract a time cycle that features ability to finish what is started. You may feel closed in, but this feeling acts as a spur to get the task completed so you can achieve greater freedom. Without the preliminary period of work, a house tends to be flimsy and can blow over quite easily. This time provides opportunity for the solid construction.

The key to this time is SATISFACTION. Where previously you might have been annoyed with work, you now gain satisfaction from a job well done. If you have been anything but pleased, turn to 4. It is likely that you will find *meaning* in what you do. That's the "chord of recognition."

Be willing to test. Spotlight the practical, discard the frills, the empty promises, the resolutions that amount to pie-in-the-sky. Under 4, you correct past errors; you avoid tripping over loose ends.

You dial 4 if you recognize the need for shoring up defenses. You recognize a need for this kind of time when you realize the necessity for cultivating a solid approach. Play time is another time; number 4 is work time. Work out details of an important project. You can be creative, because you perceive the finished product. While others might have a blind spot, might be discouraging in attitude as well as ultra-skeptical, you will continue, complete, see ahead so that the work becomes a pleasure, is meaningful and leads to future luxury.

You keep busy during this time. If you have suffered an emotional setback, this is the time for you. You get your affairs in order. You begin to watch your diet, take exercise. You are sensible, rational. You avoid extremes. Your sense of balance is enhanced; you handle assignments in a manner worthy of praise from superiors, family members, friends, loved ones. YOU CAN PROVE YOURSELF TO ONE WHO NEEDS REASSURANCE. More important, you prove your capabilities to yourself.

The temptation is to put things off, to accept sideline assignments; but, if you overcome this temptation, you dig in, get the basics accomplished and feel the glow that comes as a result. This glow can not only be emotional, but can result in financial gain.

During the 4 time you recognize LIMITATIONS. Thus you avoid overextending yourself physically and financially.

YOU WORK WITH MATERIALS AT HAND—and you work well. You exhibit your skills during this period. You organize, perform services. Rather than feeling blocked, limited, you examine obstacles and are capable of hurdling them. That's the kind of time number 4 on the Thought Dial actually represents. Is it your time? If so, dial it!

Now is the time to get rid of red tape. Cut through the nonessentials. Get to the heart of matters, not only in work, but also in personal relationships. Under 4, you are precise. You live up to obligations. Your plans are practical and you are capable of fulfilling them. You should, during this time, be aware of budget requirements without being penurious.

A promotion might occur, because those in authority are aware of your accomplishments. A raise in pay often accompanies such a period as this; but you earn it. Nothing is handed to you on a silver platter. The self-satisfaction that you experience carries over, is contagious and, very often, inspires associates and family members to live up to their own potential.

There is nothing flashy about this time. Your responsibility to children keeps you from going off to a far-away place. Your ties with friends, your promises, obligations, act as a steadying anchor. But you are not tied down; rather, you recognize needs and responsibilities and gain inwardly from meeting them.

You are, to put it plainly, dialing a time for being *conscientious*. You balance the books, repair the damage, build a system of economy, restore the faith of others— and also your own. YOU ARE DIALING A PERIOD OF SELF-DEVELOPMENT.

Credit and position are magnified here. Your plans and aspirations are concrete rather than flimsy. You are discerning, your choice is discriminating, you draw from the real rather than the fantastic. You document your opinions. You check source material. And you go directly to the source. This is an excellent time for reporting, checking, plugging the loopholes.

You learn the difference, during this time, between the monumental and the trivial. This is your time if petty details have piled up and caused you to throw up your hands in despair. Number 4 time will get those hands busy, sorting, classifying, reporting, getting thoughts and ideas on paper. A FORMAT IS PREPARED, AND IT WORKS. A

PLAN IS PRESENTED, AND IT IMPRESSES BECAUSE OF ITS SOLIDITY.

Don't dial 4 if you want to go to a party. Don't dial 4 if you want to play at working. Don't dial 4 if you feel the need of an immediate vacation. That's not what you're going to attract. What you *will* attract are conditions that enable you to build for a future vacation, a time when you are able to build for that future period when you become financially capable of throwing parties, entertaining and showing off a house built on something tangible. You don't get a house of cards here; you get one that is substantial and can withstand foul as well as fair weather.

During this time you do your homework, and the greater your preparation, the greater the chances for success. Avoid self-pity, for you asked for challenge, work, tests and trials—and that's just what you're going to get. Instead of feeling sorry for yourself, start digging in toward the goal of solid accomplishment. You will, if you respond constructively, attract friends and associates who lend a helping hand rather than drain you of resources. If this is what you need, you need this time.

This is a time when you receive valid answers, when you plant seeds that grow, when you overcome the petty and sing a song of life instead of the blues. Is this what you want and need? Does the chord of recognition sound? If so, then dial 4.

This time brings quiet confidence and establishes a solid professional and domestic base. You now become an indefatigable worker; there is drive and purpose to your efforts. It is not wise, during this time, to gamble on results. You *know* rather than contemplate; you find out rather than speculate.

IF YOU HAVE BEEN WASTING MONEY ON GAMES OF CHANCE, IF YOUR WORK HAS BEEN SHODDY, IF YOU HAVE BEEN UNDER THE INFLUENCE OF ECCENTRIC FRIENDS—then you *need* number 4.

You may wonder about the necessity for change. That may be a necessity, but *not now*. Wait, observe, calculate; piece together the details, because you are going to be called upon to recite the facts.

YOU BEGIN BUILDING A BANK ACCOUNT during this time. YOU ARE ON SCHEDULE.

YOUR ACTIONS ARE CONSERVATIVE RATHER THAN FLAM-
BOYANT.

YOUR JUDGMENT IS CORRECT RATHER THAN OFF BASE.

YOUR INTENTIONS ARE SINCERE RATHER THAN DECEP-
TIVE.

YOU ARE MODERN IN AN EFFICIENT WAY RATHER THAN IN
AN OUTLANDISH MANNER.

You, in dialing this time, are asking your subconscious
to be orderly. You are leaving behind a period filled with
activity for activity's sake. You are gaining purpose and
direction. And this brings with it a need for discipline,
work, determination. And that is just what you need if
you are dialing a 4 time.

You give and receive orders. You are perhaps blunt,
but this is because the line is straight rather than meander-
ing. There is purpose and form to this time. You are
limited, but the limitations are necessary. You require this
time if you wish to eliminate wasted motion, wasted
money, wasted time. Dial 4 for results. Dial 4 for satisfaction from work. Dial 4 to bring order out of chaos. Your
subconscious but awaits your command.

Number Five Time

When you dial number 5, you are attracting change,
travel, variety, communication with the opposite sex.
Number 5 is mercurial; it changes quickly, brings mes-
sages and concerns the written word, the sound, the call,
the message, the information, that is swift in coming and
demands instantaneous reaction.

If you are satisfied where you are and pleased with your
current way of life, stay away from 5. However, if you
seek to penetrate mysteries, if you want to know the WHY
of events, then place your Thought Dial on 5.

Number 5 is intriguing because it involves creative
thinking. In turn, creative thinking involves change. Some
of your views will undergo a transformation. What was
will no longer be. You will attract those who write, think,
oppose and rebel. Many will be born under Gemini, from
May 21 to June 20, and under the zodiacal sign of Virgo,
from August 23 to September 22.

Strive now to strike that chord of recognition. If your Thought Dial belongs on 5, you should know, perceive, understand, *see*. Are you breaking away, are you straining at the bit, are you sick of restrictions, rules, regulations; are you willing to take your chances on your own opinions, creative urges and abilities? If so, then turn to 5.

DON'T turn to 5 if you are fearful of change, if you are satisfied with the security that comes as a result of adhering to a daily routine. If merely dissatisfied, leave 5 alone.

IF YOU ARE INSISTENT ON PROBING, DEMANDING, ASKING, CRITICIZING, EVEN REBELLING IN THE SENSE THAT AUTHORITIES MUST PROVE THEMSELVES BEFORE YOU ACCEPT —then your time now is 5 and that's where your Thought Dial belongs.

With 5 fed to your subconscious, you will attract members of the opposite sex. In fact, there could be intensified relations with the opposite sex leading to marriage. If married, the 5 cycle could coincide with an addition to the family. Frankly, number 5 is one symbol that attracts sex into the life experience. But there is more to it than the physical act when you tune in this time. You draw to you *concern* with regard to a member of the opposite sex. Study the chapter "Direct Questions Answered." You will note this: ". . . the subconscious, via this symbol, reveals that creativity, including love, etc., is necessary to the solution of the problem."

When you dial you could be "calling" for marriage. You are also dialing a time for change, travel, communication of thoughts—through writing or the other arts.

Number 5 is a time when you experiment, ask questions and obtain answers. And the added information you gain is brought about through a combination of thinking, analyzing, teaching, asserting and listening.

In dialing 5 you attract a time that promotes short journeys, basic issues, attention to work, health, dealings with relatives and neighbors. This is an active time as opposed to a period of tranquillity.

If you want to write or report—5 is your time. If you want to close a shell about you, 5 is not your time. If you want to deal with emotional problems involving the opposite sex, 5 is your time. If you want to hide from basic problems, 5 is not your time. If you want to expand and experiment, 5 is your time. If you want to play it safe, 5 is not for you.

Number 5 promotes talk and other forms of communication. It also coincides with a time of travel, of journeys, of ideas. You come alive to a great extent during this period. It is a time of activity as opposed to silent acceptance. Number 5 is a promoter of self-expression. It is a confrontation with issues, including emotional ones. DO YOU WANT TO TACKLE AN EMOTIONAL RELATIONSHIP— understand where a romance is going? Then turn your Thought Dial on 5.

Are you concerned with "spreading the word"? Well, 5 is a time to advertise, promote. Your sales ability is enhanced. Communication leads to action and reaction. And when you compute this symbol into the subconscious, that is exactly what you will draw to you: a period of action, promotion, sales, advertising, dealing with the public, mostly in a written form. But you will also express your views orally. You will discuss, participate in panels both formal and informal.

Better communication with brothers and sisters is also symbolized by this time. If you have been estranged from close relatives, even neighbors, and if you want to change the situation, dial 5. If you seek greater communication, touch, feel, hearing, understanding—if you are willing to give as well as receive—then dial 5. WHEN YOU DO YOU WILL BE ACTIVE RATHER THAN INACTIVE, YOU WILL TAKE A CHANCE, YOU WILL BE SURROUNDING YOURSELF WITH ISSUES AND YOU WILL HAVE THE VITALITY WITH WHICH TO CONFRONT THEM.

You become alert. Opportunity knocks; you hear it, answer it, challenge it, ride with it, tackle it, become a part of the wave, riding with it to a final destination. You dial adventure, a clash of ideas, perhaps the excitement of self-discovery.

You magnify your COMPREHENSION during this time. You realize what is going on about you. You are *sensitive* to surroundings and events. You could become a parent during this time. You could get married. You could become involved in a romance. Whatever occurs is apt to affect you in a meaningful manner. It is not the superficial number 3; it is number 5, and you analyze, perceive, communicate, become involved.

You become a go-getter, a salesman, promoter, an instigator of action. Is this the kind of time you desire? Does this kind of time strike a chord of recognition, of need? It is a time when you must control the pace, hold the reins, otherwise you don't attract love. Instead, you are dominated by sex, the physical; you run yourself down because jealousy and insecurity gnaws away until you become a shell of your former self. Every time, it should be remembered, is two-sided, has a head and a tail, is positive and negative. Number 5 is no exception. You can dial it and get romance, a beautiful physical relationship that leads to love. But if you lack discipline, you can be dialing emotional havoc.

On the positive side you become magnetic, drawing to you persons with ideas to express, stories to write, reports to record; you find people coming into your life who have something to say, to do, a purpose for their existence, or at least an *awareness*.

YOU ARE REJUVENATED, you generate enthusiasm, you inspire, you strive and analyze and are vital enough to attract dynamic people and all this because you dial 5 and respond to the positive aspects of this time.

You write, you state your case, you let others know what you think. You declare, assert, express ideas. This is a period of action rather than delay, a time of issues rather than abstract ideas.

Dial 5 when you want to get away from details. This is the time when you whet your curiosity. Now your intellectual desire to know is spotlighted. You learn what makes people tick. In so doing you arrive at a greater degree of self-knowledge. Although some of the barriers are cracked, this is not an easy time. Effort must be expended because you are not satisfied merely to know that something occurred. You want to know *why* it happened. This takes motion, action; it requires analysis. You have to synthesize events, tie loose ends. Your mind is open to suggestion. Most importantly, you *present* ideas. You clarify thought, eradicate confusion, enable others to appreciate, learn, deduct. You write, read; you advertise and communicate. You put on paper the words and thoughts in your mind. Number 5 is not an easy time, because the world of ideas is exhausting. But it is also *invigorating*. Is this the kind of time you now *need*?

You talk, speak, announce. There is repartee. Life becomes more of an adventure; this being the case, you take chances. If you need security, skip 5. If you need spark, change, travel, confrontation with problems, dilemmas, puzzles, then you want 5.

Under 5 you obtain a fresh point of view. You see persons, situations, from a different angle. The excitement of discovery is present. WHAT YOU KNOW IS NO LONGER OLD HAT. WHAT YOU KNOW BECOMES MORE VALID BECAUSE YOU UNDERSTAND AS WELL AS KNOW. You come to *recognize* as well as to be familiar. Number 5 time is provocative; you are restless, keen to experience, hungry to add to knowledge. You gain insight and provide this ingredient for others.

IF YOU WANT TO WRITE . . . dial 5.

IF YOU WANT TO TRAVEL . . . dial 5.

IF YOU WANT ROMANCE . . . dial 5.

IF YOU WANT TO COMMUNICATE . . . dial 5.

IF YOU WANT BETTER RELATIONS WITH BROTHERS, SISTERS . . . dial 5.

IF YOU WANT GREATER UNDERSTANDING WITH CO-WORKERS . . . dial 5.

IF YOU WANT TO TAKE STEPS TOWARD SELF-IMPROVEMENT . . . dial 5.

Remember, however, that in so doing you are taking upon yourself the challenge of *enlightenment*. This means that you change your ways. You discard old habits. You go through the discomfort of tossing aside preconceived notions. You become creative through change. The comfort of staying put is no longer present. There is the whirl of activity and travel. And the world around you no longer is open to investigation and experiment. If this is not truly "your time" it would be a grievous mistake to dial it.

With freedom, there is also responsibility. Perhaps, unless you thoroughly understand what you are asking for (dialing), you are less free than otherwise with this kind of "freedom." Actually, you are asking for the freedom to be responsible, to express, to discourse, to take upon your shoulders the weight of another's life and love. Now, are you still positive that the 5 time should be your time?

DIAL 5 AND GET READY TO DISCARD THE OLD.

DIAL 5 AND BE READY FOR MEANINGFUL CHANGE.

DIAL 5 AND ATTRACT THE OPPOSITE SEX.

DIAL 5 FOR LOVE, FREEDOM, TRAVEL, EXCITEMENT, DISCOVERY.

DIAL 5 AND BE READY FOR THE NEED TO BE RESOURCE-
FUL, VERSATILE.

DIAL 5 AND REALIZE YOU CAN'T BE NERVOUS, INDECISIVE
OR RECKLESS.

DIAL 5 AND PREPARE FOR THE PRESSURE OF TAKING CARE
NOT ONLY OF YOURSELF BUT OF THOSE YOU HAVE IN-
FLUENCED, ATTRACTED, WON OVER. You are dialing a time
for self-realization. And when you know yourself, you will
not be satisfied to live only for yourself.

If this is the kind of change you want, then your
Thought Dial should be on 5.

Number Six Time

You dial this time, basically, when you are ready to
change residence or make domestic adjustments. Number
6 time is a period when you seek harmony. It is a time
associated with money, collections, partnerships, legal
affairs, marriage, public relations. Dialing number 6 brings
you in contact with persons born under Taurus, from
April 20 to May 20, and Libra, from September 23 to
October 22.

What happens during this time cycle adds up to a
change in the home situation. Number 6 time also brings
about a greater appreciation of the arts, of music, and, at
times, encourages an individual to try singing. IF YOU ARE
CONCERNED WITH YOUR VOICE, IF YOU WANT TO IMPROVE
YOUR MUSICAL TECHNIQUE, dial 6. If you want "harmony"
within the family circle, dial 6. YOU DISCOVER OR REDIS-
COVER LOVED ONES DURING THIS TIME PERIOD; you straight-
en out family differences.

Artistic expression is encouraged; you find that the
obstacles are not so large, that the opposition tends to
melt. These are the conditions you attract when the
Thought Dial is placed on number 6. This is the information you are storing in the subconscious, and, as a result,
the subconscious get busy, just as a computer would come
up with the answers if it were fed the correct information.

During this period you are appreciative of luxury, art
objects and music. And you begin, perhaps as a hobby, to
strive for personal artistic expression. A professional in this

field, dialing 6, can help you discover a unique outlet, can perfect techniques, can add to chances for success.

You desire luxury items and want to beautify your home. The key is not to get in over your head. Buy, but do so in a sensible manner.

Dialing number 6 attracts improved conditions at home. It could also be a time when you have a home of your own through marriage, a home through purchase. The emphasis, the spotlight, is on domestic conditions and, if this is what you desire, dial 6.

ADJUSTMENTS are made during this time—and, during number 6 time, there is a settling down where domestic affairs are concerned. You are able to *delineate* your responsibilities. You discover your own; you shake off those you might have assumed that do not belong to you. That's what you attract when you implant 6 in your subconscious. You become the homemaker. You find your time taken up with family affairs; you mature in the sense that you know where you belong, what must be accomplished.

IF IT IS EXCITEMENT AND CHANGE YOU SEEK, THIS IS NOT YOUR TIME. BUT IF YOU WANT TO CONCENTRATE YOUR EFFORTS IN AREAS OF FAMILY REUNION, UNDERSTANDING OF LOVED ONES, MORE PEACE AT HOME, MORE BEAUTY IN YOUR SURROUNDINGS, WELL-BEING, THEN THIS IS YOUR TIME.

Sense of duty, responsibility, come surging to the forefront. No longer do you want to be here, there and everywhere. YOU WANT TO BE AT HOME. You want your surroundings to be familiar, you want to belong. And in so desiring, your subconscious gets busy and attracts those conditions.

With 6, home becomes the center of efforts, affection. The home is beautified. A disturbing influence is removed. You are better able to meet obligations. When you dial 6 you are attracting a time when you tend to want to fix things *your way*. On the negative side, this could result in meddlesome action on your part. Beware of this. Respect your family members, be as polite to them as you would be to strangers. You are in a position to attract music, harmony, happiness; it is up to you to recognize these positive aspects when they are encountered. You also attract a greater sense of justice and, very often, greater earning capacity.

You add to your income by dealing directly with the

public, by avoiding middlemen, by selling your own product and your unique ideas.

Face the fact that you're going to have more responsibility. BUT YOU WILL BE RESPONSIBLE FOR THE THINGS YOU BELIEVE IN. YOU WILL BE RESPONSIBLE TO THOSE YOU LOVE. YOU WILL BE RESPONSIBLE IN THE SENSE THAT A FAMILY AND HOME REMAIN BECAUSE OF YOUR EFFORTS.

Do you want greater contentment? Then dial 6. Do you want to bask in the warmth of affection? Then dial 6. Are you willing to give up some superficial interests for the greater good of the home unit? Then dial 6. This kind of time calls for a thorough approach, demands conscientiousness on your part.

IF YOU WANT BETTER HOME AND MARRIAGE CONDITIONS, get that dial on 6. You become more reliable because you are in a better position to accomplish, succeed. You bring with you an inner peace because that is what will result during the positive aspects of the 6 time. People want you around, and you desire to be wanted; and so there is mutual satisfaction.

Specifically, if you want to purchase a home, to change your residence, if you seek a reunion with a mate, if you want to enhance emotional and financial security, you need 6. Dial it! Study these words for that chord of recognition. If it strikes, if you see it and hear it, you can know that dialing 6 is what you require.

You attract to yourself weddings, and activity in community affairs. You become aware of design, music, art. You take better care of personal appearance and general surroundings. You do things with color. Interior decorating intrigues you. You strive for understanding of subtle nuances of sound, environment. You tend, also, to indulge yourself. This could place a strain on the budget. It is all part of the number 6 picture: the fireplace, the piano, the painting, the home, the family, the luxury item and the love.

You rent, sign a lease, purchase, build. YOUR EVENINGS ARE MORE LIKELY TO BE SPENT AT HOME THAN ELSEWHERE. You give advice without attempting to force ideas on others. You gain more through diplomacy than by trying to use direct methods. People with family problems come to you because they sense you have been through them and have emerged victorious. This being the case, keep your guard up lest you become involved in problems that belong to others. Give freely, but don't try to shove your own methods to the fore; instead, give with the knowledge that your advice may not be acted upon. But the fact that you care enough to *offer* has a constructive effect. Number 6 gets you involved, but draw the line when it comes to intruding. WAIT TO BE ASKED. Keep the door to your conciliation services open, but don't attempt to drag anyone inside, especially your family and close friends. You gain through patience. You gain, during this period, by being friendly. You lose if you are impatient, insistent, demanding. Many want to lean on you in order to obtain a breathing spell. Many never really mean to follow your advice, but they end up doing so.

Number 6 brings activity with groups such as the Parent-Teachers Association; gets you involved in community projects and with school programs. You are concerned with the security of your family, but you are also in tune with requirements for the welfare of others.

You attract to yourself the cares of others. In this new-found sense of responsibility, you are apt to take on more than can be intelligently handled. Don't permit this to occur. You want your family and you want to make people happy. But, in so desiring, don't become a doormat. Draw a line—one side is responsibility and the other side is "being used." Don't permit others to exploit you. Volunteer your services and advice, but don't permit others to take you for granted. Radiate a sense of security, but don't permit others to think of you as a money tree. This is a delicate time because you attract envy. People oppose you just to see if they can shake your air of tranquillity. Be peaceful without being complacent. Be happy without losing your sense of challenge. Appreciate friends and family, but also hold a high regard for yourself. Spotlight self-esteem. If you like yourself, you can also like others. If you feel unworthy, others will perceive this and treat you accordingly.

Start reacting in a positive manner by being conscious of personal appearance. If you are indifferent, others interpret this as a sign that you don't deserve any better. When you dial 6, you dial a time when the better you treat yourself the better others will treat you. You are dialing a time when you require the respect of those closest to you. You get it by first respecting yourself. In so doing, you set in motion a chain reaction. Others respect you, family conditions improve, the home becomes your base of operations, you achieve greater tranquillity. This is what you need, especially at home, if you are dialing 6.

During this time your family becomes a friend. Amusements are shared. Past conflict tends to evaporate. You can entertain during this time, especially at home. You can prosper because you get the backing of the people who mean the most to you. There certainly is an increase in psychic income, greater satisfaction from what you do.

You dial 6 when you want to do business in connection with decorating, with home, with luxury items. You dial this number when you want to activate interest in music, art, poetry, sculpturing, painting. IF YOU ARE GOING INTO AN AREA OF INVESTMENT OR ACTIVITY CONNECTED WITH PERFUME, dial 6. Personal adornments, incense, products that bring joy and require discernment, appreciation— these require the 6 time to be activated.

Dial 6 when you want to mediate a dispute. Work, labor unions, management relations—these areas also require the diplomatic force represented by 6. You're going to get beauty with 6, but there is also power and a need to be responsible. You're not dialing a "lark." Instead, you're computing into your subconscious a pattern which sees you taking on the burden of supporting a family emotionally and financially. You are going to have to inspire in others appreciation for the finer points, the good life, the beauty of surroundings, the difference between luxury and mere ostentatiousness. You are indeed dialing a time when child's play is over. Realize this before placing the Thought Dial on 6. Otherwise the home places you in debt, the luxury becomes agony, the family becomes a burden, the harmony becomes dull, the hearth becomes a bore.

THIS IS THE TIME FOR GIVING AND RECEIVING GIFTS. You also can hire people to work in your home; you now seem to have a knack for picking the right persons for duties connected with your residence.

Number 6 is basically a time for renewing friendships, for gaining domestic peace, for taking upon yourself the right and responsibility to turn your house into a palace. Simply put, if you want home and marriage, this is your number. If you desire escapades, the excitement of roaming, making conquests, get off 6.

Be generous but guard possessions. You attract rare

objects, books, but also those who would like to relieve you of them. Encourage within yourself a sense of balance. Collect but don't burden yourself with too many possessions. If you do, you will be possessed by them.

By now you are familiar with what 6 brings. Dial it if it has what you require at this time.

Number Seven Time

You dial number 7 when, basically, you are concerned with working behind the scenes. Number 7 is Neptune and television, motion pictures, radio, with being behind the microphone, behind the camera; that is, you can be seen and heard, but it is basically a dealing with illusion. You are seen on the motion-picture screen, you are heard on the air, your image is imposed on the TV screen but you are not there in person.

Number 7 time brings you in contact with persons born under Pisces, from February 19 to March 20. When you place the Thought Dial on 7 you must take care to avoid self-deception. You must make an effort to see persons, situations as they actually exist. The temptation is to envision people, places and events as you wish they could be. Why, then, would you want this kind of time? You would want it if you appreciate privacy. You need 7 time to discover that being alone is not the same as being lonely. Number 7 brings you in contact with yourself. It is a time of self-discovery. It is not an easy time in the sense that everything is smooth. Number 7, being Neptune, is associated with the Twelfth House, symbolizing hospitals, clubs, groups and organizations.

Are you weary of the hurly-burly of the so-called rat race? If so, dial 7. Do you yearn, now, for the beauty of nature, for the perfection of knowing who you are, where you are going? Then dial 7. Number 7 gives a drive for perfection. There cannot be a real wrong when you are right wtih yourself. Is there a chord of recognition here? Do you perceive a need? Then it is 7 time for you.

This point on the dial is not popular. It is special. Dial it for motion-picture or television. Dial it when you want to tune in on yourself. If it is psychic experience you seek, dial 7. If you are concerned with extrasensory experience, mediumistic work, dial 7. You would dial 8 for more materialistic purposes. You dial 7 for a spiritual adventure. NUMBER 7 COULD BRING YOU FACE TO FACE WITH SECRET FEARS. Number 7 time is a period when you walk into the empty closet to make sure it really contains nothing to fear. Number 7 takes you back to a time when you feared the dark, the unknown. It brings the unknown closer, close enough to examine.

YOU RIGHT THE WORLD IN YOUR OWN MIND when you dial 7. You realize that many flaws and fears exist only in your mind. Number 7, perhaps more than any other time, demands patience. You wait, you observe, you perceive. Not a time for contracts, commitments. You are straightening yourself out, getting rid of emotional kinks. You are, during this time, finding out what it is you realy desire.

Number 7 is excellent for institutional work, for association with hospitals. ARE YOU PUZZLED ABOUT A RELATIONSHIP? Then dial 7. If you do, your subconscious is instructed to wait, to analyze, to seek the favorable and unfavorable in a dispassionate manner. You could get at the truth during this time, no matter how painful. But the 7 time, the "truth time," could make you free. There is greater freedom of decision because the load of commitment and responsibility, real, or imagined, is lifted. If you feel you have been too hurried and harried, dial 7. You will thus provide yourself with a breathing spell, with time to evaluate and decide.

When you dial 7 you learn to be alone WITHOUT SUFFERING PANGS OF LONELINESS. This is a time to reject the false, no matter how attractive the bait. This is a time to grasp truth, no matter how difficult this might appear. You evaluate without the illusion of perfection. You find that people and situations need not be perfect to be useful, constructive, satisfying. You leave an adolescent period; sophomoric desires go by the wayside in favor of a mature choice. That's number 7, if you're ready for it.

You eliminate from your area of consciousness unessential persons and things; you trim down to the essentials. You get close to your own nature and, in so doing, extend your capability of understanding to other areas. The axiom of "physician, heal thyself" becomes a working one. "Know thyself" becomes a working philosophy.

Much of what you held essential is broken down. A

period of *devolution* occurs, to be followed by personal *evolution*. You become close to nature; you observe trees, fish; you imitate nature. You understand the realities and come to a close understanding of your own emotions, personality, mentality, motive. THERE IS A CULMINATION OF WHAT HAS BEEN—THERE IS A BEGINNING OF WHAT IS TO BE.

You deal with judges, you could be involved in court; decisions, justice, perfection, invention, patents, government papers are all part of this number 7 time period.

If you want to be at the forefront, however, this is not your time. If, on the other hand, you are willing to lie back, to wait, to be patient, to be a force BEHIND THE SCENES, this *is* your time.

You find how deep your emotions run during this period. You find your own depth. You get at the truth. There is illusion, beauty; and also on the positive side is an ability to separate truth from falsehood, reality from illusion. Obviously this is no time to play with. Number 7 time is, if nothing else, a serious period. There is none of the number 3 superficiality about this time.

When you dial 7 you attract psychic experiences. You seem able to perceive, to know, to determine, when something of importance is about to occur. Knowing this, knowing that you will *know*, you don't disturb yourself about the nonessentials, about the unimportant. You dial 7 to bring about a period of silence, of introspection. You live within and learn to understand the mechanics of yourself: what makes you joyful, sad, indifferent or enthusiastic.

If you want to get away from it all, this is your time—IF you know why you want privacy. That is, number 7 should not be dialed for mere escapism. If you know that you want time to think, to analyze, to perfect, to synthesize various elements of your life—if that's the kind of getting away—then it is time for 7.

This is, in effect, a secretive time. It is a time when your individuality shines through: you work as an individual, you plan individually, you separate from the crowd and you may appear to be a lonely figure. This attracts envy because many, many persons want to know themselves but lack the courage to do so. Dialing 7 gives you a spiritual insight that, ordinarily, is elusive, almost impossible to capture.

In dialing 7 you bring upon yourself a period when you appear reticent. You want to express yourself, but you want to do it with *perfection*. So, on the negative side, you hesitate to try at all. On a positive level, you do try because you know the perfection must come from within, not from external forms of expression. You are selective during this period. You want the best; you desire the unique and you attract to you special experiences and persons.

Dial 7 for MEDITATION. You get to the bottom of the mystery that is you with this time. This is a period for research, for perfecting techniques, skills. It is not enough to *want;* it is necessary to *train*. By dialing 7 your subconscious is programmed to discipline your talents, desires, mode of expression. Out of this discipline comes a style. Out of this period of being alone emerges the professional as differentiated from the enthusiastic, but bumbling amateur. That's why this time is discipline, training.

This is a *subjective* time. You look out from within. Everything comes from what you feel; objectivity is not this time. If you want to be objective, dial another time. When you dial 7 you will be subjective, but your emotions will be under control. Number 7 is spiritual, religious in the sense that you respect nature, that you seek greater understanding of what it is that maintains the orderliness of the solar system. YOU BECOME A SEEKER. You train to be a specialist. This is especially favorable for hospital work or efforts connected with helping others to regain their health. For a doctor who embarks on a research project—a project requiring an almost recluselike existence combined with scientific discipline—number 7 is the right time. For any individual who is willing to delve into the mysteries of life, number 7 is the right time. It is not for the dilettante; it is deep, serious, and penetrates beneath layers of pretense.

Number 7 time is excellent for buying and selling real estate. This is a good time for metaphysical writing and publishing. It is excellent for religious training. You understand various religions and perceive the truth about the history of religion during this time. You transcend petty prejudice. You grow because you begin to see a pattern unfold in history and within yourself.

For clandestine affairs, secret meetings, negotiations, discreet encounters, dial 7.

Achieve greater mental balance during this time. Achieve it or suffer the consequences. Your imagination, if permitted to run wild, will control you and bury you. That's the danger of this time. You worry that control is lacking. You imagine yourself a messiah; you feel persecuted when you lose control during this period. It is, as stated, not a time to "play with", it is a time for discipline, for you are entering depths that include psychic experience and self-examination.

This is a time to choose a field of specialized endeavor. Sharpen your technique. Avoid shoddy persons and methods. Overcome temptation to take the easy way. Avoid get-rich-quick schemes. During this time they represent ways of becoming poor—fast. Heed your intuition. Heed the voice within. Don't battle your conscience. You won't win. Follow its dictates. It leads you along a path of fulfillment. And that is what you are seeking at this time, or you would not have dialed 7.

This is a time for reflection. Dial something else for quick change, spectacular results or entertainment. Number 7 is not any of those times. It is for perfecting, honing to razor-sharpness your specialized talents.

You will get money if you don't strain for it. Rather, *wait* for developments. Don't submit anything that does not represent your best work.

This is a time for *inspiration*. You are inspired when you dial 7; and if this is so, if the chord of recognition has struck, you are on your right time.

Number Eight Time

You dial this number for business, for responsibility, for greater authority and the rewards that accompany power; for executive positions, for investment, emotional involvement, including relations with the opposite sex that could lead to marriage or, if married, to an addition to the family. Number 8 is associated with Saturn and the Tenth House. Dialing it brings you in contact with individuals born under Capricorn, from December 22 to January 19.

Dial 8 to elevate standing in the community, to enhance prestige, to fulfill aspirations. Dial it when you are willing to make sacrifices in order to further ambitions. Number 8 is drive, the past, dealing with other individuals.

This is your Thought Dial number if you have been asking for an opportunity, backing, or if you are investing time and money to put a pet theory to work. It is excellent for ATTRACTING INVESTORS. Number 8 helps you inspire confidence. It is conservative; but, when you dial 8, you have to be ready to back words with actions. You will be called upon to be tough, to hire and fire, decide whether to accept or reject.

If you really mean business, if this strikes that chord of recognition, number 8 time is now your time. However, to "mean business" spreads to various areas: seriousness about a relationship, seriousness of purpose in organizing, in dispensing rules and regulations, in setting up a corporation, in striving to succeed in a competitive career. DON'T DIAL 8 IF YOU ARE INDIFFERENT ABOUT PURPOSE, IF YOU ARE APT TO CHANGE YOUR MIND OR IF YOU ARE SIMPLY EXPERIMENTING AND TRYING TO FIND YOUR WAY. Number 8 time gets thoroughly involved—*and the ties are binding*.

During 8 time, past efforts pay dividends. Your selection of stocks is apt to be excellent *for the long-range pull*.

Dial 8 for going into business for yourself. Dial 8 for marriage. Dial 8 for a virile approach that marks you as an individual with confidence. Dial 8 when you are positive that you intend to stick, that you are here to stay rather than to vacillate.

Dial 8 for commerce, or when willing to assume added responsibility, pressure. Number 8 time could bring money and power but, with it, you also get a feeling of restriction. If you are careless you could get in over your head.

If you have something to sell to an organization, a large corporation, get in on number 8 time. If you want to deal with the *individual,* you would dial 1. If you want to perform public service or promote institutional advertising, you would dial 9. Number 8 time is strictly for business *on a large scale*.

Want to convince a bank or other lending agency that you have the goods, that you can deliver? Then dial 8. This feeds into your subconscious the "order" to organize, to prepare to utilize past experience, to put forth an image of conservatism, responsibility—one that inspires faith in those who have capital to risk or provide.

During 8 time you deal with goods, material; you are worldly rather than spiritual, you seek power rather than solace. When you place the Thought Dial on 8 you are attracting people connected with business, with executive positions, those with the authority to make decisions affecting huge sums of money. Is this what you want? Be sure, or you may find yourself feeling limited, locked in, closed up, tied down, pressured to such an extent that you throw all responsibility aside and overreact in the opposite direction. You move with precision; the rhythm is steady rather than wild, even rather than imaginative. The course is straight up, with no sideline for amusement.

Number 8 time brings you in contact with the executive, the leader, the business magnate, the person who puts up the money—or takes it away. Number 8, on a personal level, intensifies relations with people, especially the opposite sex. It is drive, virility; but it isn't play. It's serious. It's marriage and children and domicile. It's protection and an economy of action, emotion. It's straight-to-the-point and lacking in the social graces, in romance. If the latter is what you seek, get on 3 or 5. Leave 8 time alone if you want to play games, want to find a frivolous outlet for your sex drive. Number 8 makes you pay for actions; it produces a Karmic cause and effect, action and reaction. You don't get away with anything during 8 time. And on the reverse side, you gain as a result of efforts, you pull yourself to the top; the drive, power and energy are well extended if you are serious. You manage, you direct, you make value judgments, you balance and you analyze.

Has that chord of recognition sounded yet? If not, then 8 is not your time—not yet, anyway. If it *has* sounded, then place your Thought Dial on 8. It will bring recognition, the authority to direct; you will be giving rather than receiving order. But don't complain about overtime, avoid gripes about extra duties. Don't indulge in the luxury of self-pity.

When you dial 8 you are informing your subconscious, directing it, to bring you money and material power. You are conditioning yourself to be steady, dependable; you will be setting an example, taking the lead, cooperating in community projects, setting yourself up in business, risking capital on your talent, judgment, product.

Dialing 8 means you are computerizing into your subconscious an attitude of confidence, tact, vision, respect for authority and experience. You will be dealing with older individuals: the head of an organization, the head of a family, the director, the organizer.

DURING THIS TIME INSPIRATION IS TRANSFORMED INTO PRACTICAL MEASURES. NOW YOU STOP TALKING ABOUT WHAT YOU WOULD LIKE TO DO. YOU GET BUSY AND YOU DO IT.

There is little or nothing that is halfway during the 8 time; it is all the way or nothing. You do not merely get your feet wet; you take the complete plunge. Certainly this is no time to shirk responsibility. You will be called upon to make the payment, put in the time, organize the effort, capitalize the project. Are you ready for this time?

If you are seeking marriage to a stable partner, if you seek security over romance, dependability over attractive promise, then dial 8. If you want a business as well as a marriage partner, your time is 8 time.

If you recognize in these words a picture of your current needs, desires: if you are *driven* in this direction, dial 8. This is a power time and the buzz of activity can be heard above all else—above relaxation, above play, above romantic love, above hobby, above social activity. Number 8 time is branching-out time in that you seek to accomplish, to build, to climb to the pinnacle. You gather forces and facts, allies and investors, organizers and promoters. You *compel* important people to cooperate. You offer something of value and your product is snapped up as a hungry animal would snap at a delicious morsel.

You deal with steel products, with lead; you organize groups, get capital together and make just decisions. Your fuel, during this time, is power, ambition, a sexual drive that brings fulfillment and causes you to accept the responsibilities of power and indulgence. You delegate duties where details are concerned. You conquer the fear of being replaced. You settle for nothing but quality. You insist on lasting value. You free yourself of money worries because you know you can produce. You are aware of time; you bring time in as your ally. You utilize your own experience and that of others. You are progressive without being reckless. You are the opposite of superficial. You are thorough; you put together the bits and pieces until a whole product emerges. That's the kind of atmosphere you are dialing.

Emphasis during this time is on finance, on an additional mouth to feed, an additional responsibility to carry. A keynote during this time is *ambition*. Dial 8 for fulfilling ambitions. Dial 8 for finding an outlet for drives, ambitions, desires. Dial 8 for meeting a challenge. Dial 8 for business. Dial 8 for a serious relationship. Dial 8 when you want to convince a captain of industry that you have the goods and can deliver them on time.

This is the time for FULL-TIME work, for effort. You become devoted to a project, an individual, a way of life. You invest and mature, you meet the challenge and accept the responsibility. You deal with pressure groups and display your power. You organize and back up assertions with cash on the barrelhead. You're not playing; you're striving, driving, pushing, building. That's your time if you place the Thought Dial on 8. You get nothing for nothing during this time. You work, achieve, create.

Dial 8 for a reward based on careful planning, research, to conclude a business transaction, or to garner wisdom based on experience. Dial 8 for marriage and offspring. Dial 8 for the patience to hang on, to have faith, to be resourceful enough to make yourself and product attractive, desirable, *needed*.

You reconstruct. You are practical, earthy. You deal in land and the produce of the earth.

YOU DIAL 8 TO ATTRACT AN AGREEMENT, A CONTRACT OF FAR-REACHING AND LONG-RANGE EFFECT.

You deal here with business leaders. You make a bid for power, authority. You take on your shoulders the responsibility of directing, organizing, investing. Now you organize your efforts, you focus your attention, pinpoint ambitions, rise to a position of leadership in the community. Does this appeal to you, or does it *frighten* you? If the latter, get off 8! If the former, set your Thought Dial on 8 and keep it there until the results flow, until the power is felt, until the position is established and the policy is set.

Form an image of your aim. Picture your goal. See yourself in a position of authority. Know that the deal will go through, that the proposition will succeed—*and turn your Thought Dial to* 8.

Get your feet on the ground. Be practical. Don't make promises that are based on wishful thinking. An affair of the heart, if pursued during 8 time, culminates in a permanent alliance. But you don't immediately run off on a honeymoon. Instead you begin putting plans into action and you find yourself a partner in business as well as in the household.

You have the power to deal justly with opposition. You welcome competition because it helps sharpen your own technique, procedure. When you dial 8, you tune in on a world of commerce—a busy and rewarding time.

You possess sufficient funds and the emotional fortitude to drive ahead in the face of opposition.

You believe in yourself.

Number Nine Time

Dial number 9 when you want to finish, complete. This is your time for spreading influence, for expanding your sphere of interest and activity. When you place your Thought Dial on 9 you attract persons born under Aries, from March 21 to April 19. You may feel the loss of the past, but you are preparing for new beginnings. Number 9 brings people to you with their problems. You are consulted, leaned upon; the key is to avoid having others merely use you.

You dial 9 when you feel something has gone out of your life, to relieve a vacuum. You computer this time into your subconscious when you are ready, when you feel *impelled* to leave the past, to terminate a relationship, when you know that the time has come to expand, to be universal, to enlarge your vision and to thrust forward to greater experience.

Now is the time for the big project; now is the time to put aside petty jealousy, minor fears and to strike ahead for bigger game. Number 9 is associated with Mars and the First House; it is indicative of initiative, personality, appeal. The effect appears to be magnetic, for people are drawn to you. There is a universal appeal about this symbol; it is excellent for institutional advertising and public relations. It has to do with the long pull rather than with short-range or quick results. You dial 9 when you are building a reputation, when you are stressing integrity, quality and lasting power.

Are you fed up with limitations, artificial barriers? Then dial 9. Do you wish to expand, to see ahead and to envision full potential? Then dial 9. Also when you are appearing before the public, convincing others that what you have to offer will be around for a long time, and is reliable, not flashy and superficial.

You take a world-wide view with 9. You dial 9 to complete, you dial 1 to start. You dial 5 for quick communication, you dial 9 for lasting impact. You dial 3 for superficial, light-hearted pleasure. You dial 9 when you are ready to assume responsibility for the well-being of large groups. You have personal pleasure with 3; you *provide* pleasure for others during the 9 time.

A chapter has been completed, the pages closed. Now you seek to make a fresh imprint and so you dial 9. But leave this time alone if your motives are basically selfish. The gain here takes time and preperation. Your vision must be sharp, unimpaired by petty fear, envy or avarice. You are, with 9, the artist, the philanthropist, the altruist—excellent for charity drives, fund-raising campaigns. Number 9 time gives you the ability to *appeal* in a creative manner. You get results when the appeal is for a cause, rather than for a personal reason, or for individual advancement. A cause, a group, an *ideal*, is furthered during this time.

Are you ready to take stock of possessions, desires, motives, ambitions, goals, aspirations, people? Then you are ready for number 9 time. Evaluate relationships. Stop seeing that individual who wastes your time and does little else. Devote yourself to a cause, a project. Aim high, stick to principles, stand tall, lead the way to accomplishment by discarding wasteful methods, negative concepts. Unless you are so prepared, steer clear of 9. It is the finish of the old, the putting away of toys, the beginning of mature concepts, drives.

Take inventory, utilize knowledge, learn lessons of value, seek greater understanding, get in tune with the "universal mind." Be a humanitarian rather than a warrior; fight for what you believe to be right, but avoid battling for petty gains. You are, when tuned in on number 9 time, about to close a chapter and to put aside mistakes, ugliness, abrasive actions. You are opening a chapter on greater understanding; your powers are *creative* rather than destructive. You meet people who are pioneers, who have dreams that can be transformed into realities with your help, with you on the ground floor, climbing and

building to a peak of solid accomplishment. A concrete,
tangible program is the result of firm efforts when you
dial 9 and inform the subconscious that the pattern has
been set and that you are going to touch the conscience of
many rather than appeal to the shallow wants of the few.

Dismiss hate; emphasize love and hope. Number 9 is
that kind of time. You have to feel yourself a big person
to invite this kind of climate. There is, during this time,
sacrifice and reward, acceptance and rejection, an end
and a beginning.

Have you gone through a divorce? Are you bitter,
lonely? Then dial 9 for a closed chapter and the light of
new hope, new starts, a beginning toward renewed
growth.

Are you caught up in a cause? Do you want to expand
horizons, heal the sick, help the emotionally wounded?
Then 9 is your time for concrete results. Nine time is
idealism; it is a spreading of the wings to shelter the
aimless, the hopeless, the forlorn. It is charity from the
heart in contrast to reluctantly giving out of a sense of
duty.

In addressing yourself to the larger picture, don't neglect personal friends. You cannot shirk duty or obligations to those close to you by claiming to be involved with
more important concerns. Balance is necessary during this
time lest you find yourself big in a sense that leaves you,
during the still, small hours, feeling quite little and lonely.
Don't overlook the *minutes* while waiting for the *hour* to
strike.

Old stumbling blocks may reappear. This time, however, you have the experience to hurdle them. You have the
courage to meet the challenge, to succeed where you may
have failed in the past: in duties, commitments, personal
relationships, campaigns to achieve an ideal.

During this time you cultivate your tastes; your sense of
appreciation for the arts is enhanced, including music and
writing. You could publish in the sense that your ideas—
and ideals—reach a larger audience.

You complete organizational plans. Your work is on a
large rather than small scale. Does this strike a chord of
yearning, longing, recognition? If so, then dial 9, for you
have approached the time for *that* time.

But if what you have read so far frightens you, leaves

you cold, strikes you as a stranger to your goals, then you have not yet arrived at the number 9 time.

You must be ready to make some personal sacrifices here for the good of family, neighbors, humanity in general. This is a big and generous operation; it calls for a bold stroke, a direct commitment, a real *desire* to finish with the shoddy, the wasteful. The need is for determination to rid the garden of weeds no matter how back-breaking a job that entails. Are you ready? Then place your Thought Dial on 9.

During the 9 time you gain opportunity for greater self-expression because you attract, as friends and allies, artists and inspirational people. You give of yourself and, in return, you receive much—in wisdom, ambition, maturity, growth as a person.

You break away from the old; your life takes a new direction and gains added purpose. Are you satisfied with the status quo? Is your personal life one of fulfillment? If so, turn away from 9. But if the opposite is true, you need this time.

What kind of time is 9? It is a period when a break occurs; it is a time when you carry a burden that rightfully is your own, not someone else's, someone who uses you and makes you feel it is a duty to lighten another's load. This is a time when the burden you carry is humanitarian, not one that is carried merely to "buy" love, not one that assures that another is dependent upon you. Can you understand? If so, you may be ready for this time.

Dial 9 for a new approach, for an end to indecision. Dial this numerical symbol for fresh viewpoints, artistic endeavors, completion of projects, a universal outlook.

This is the time to advertise, to inaugurate a public-relations program, to publish and disseminate information. You become the doctor, nurse, teacher; you break through to a direction leading to greater freedom, peace of mind, *inner satisfaction*.

Remove yourself as a crutch for those who refuse to help themselves. During this time you have the courage to be compassionate, but in such a manner as to promote greater independence in those you have been aiding. Journeys of the mind are indicated, and this could lead to actual journeys, real ones, a moving ahead, an enlarging, new experiences, and the end of a time when your purpose was to be used, leaned upon, abused. It could mark the end of a business or personal relationship—and that's the kind of time that attracts you to number 9. You dial this symbol because you recognize the need for realization that a new time is approaching and that old ways are going by the wayside. It is not an easy time, because a breakup is seldom pretty. But it is a *necessary* time.

You express in a large way during this time; the canvas of your efforts is big, the strokes are bold. You set into motion a lightning chain of good will. You travel wide and you heal; you are called upon for appearances and the *recognition* you receive is quite different from previous times, when some selfish, thoughtless individuals caused you to lean backward and act as a mere stepping-stone for their desires. Can you perceive this meaning? If so, dial 9. Dial 9 for greater self-expression, for organizing and building in a sense that touches the minds, the hearts, the needs, of many rather than the few. *Dedication of purpose* goes hand-in-hand with this time. DON'T dial it if your thinking and feeling remains small, petty, fearful.

You are *selfless*. You give freely. You are heartened when one who is ill shows signs of recovery. *And in so giving, in so loving, you attract love.*

If you finally have decided on this kind of time, if you want the kind of love that this time generates—dial 9.

Number 9 time gets your message across through publications, via the mail, through broad contacts.

Dial 9 for that advertising campaign and good will program. Dial 9 to promote institutions that benefit many, for this, eventually, will accrue benefits to you.

That's the kind of time you attract when the Thought Dial is on 9.

Number Eleven Time

Number 11 is associated with Uranus, which symbolizes astrology and the mantic arts-sciences. Number 11, and Uranus, have to do with friends, hopes and wishes, and are associated with the Eleventh House—a section of the chart that accents friendships, has to do with romantic interests and finally tells the story of whether one's desires are to be fulfilled. Turning the Thought Dial to 11 brings

Uranian interests into your life: astrology, ESP, psychic phenomena, numerology, etc. With 11 on my dial, I almost immediately received television offers connected with astrology and drew assignments for books on astrology. That's what I would call instantaneous response!

You dial 11 when you are ready for sudden events, changes, challenges: you dial 11 when you are ready to teach, to share knowledge, to trade and expand. The Uranian nature of this symbol tells your subconscious to gird for the unusual, the unexpected, the sudden action—it is divorce from the status quo, a war with the establishment, a stating of principles in a manner such as to attract valuable allies and help fulfill ultimate objectives.

You don't dial 11 when you want to travel the beaten path, to take the tried-and-true course. You ignore 11 when you want the orthodox. You DO dial 11 when you want to attract to you persons born under Aquarius, from January 20 to February 18. You DO dial 11 when it is aviation, television (in a different aspect than under 7 time), electricity, magnetism, the experiment, the thrust into strange, nearly occult areas that you desire. You are asking to become a master in your field. You are computerizing your subconscious to set you on a path that leads to the exotic, the mysterious; it is also a path filled with pitfalls and, unless balance is maintained, brilliance degenerates into mere eccentricity.

You dial 11 when "ready" for sudden change; there is divorce from usual activities. This is a cut-off period; you lose what you had but you gain an electric-current kind of life. What was is no more; in its place is a buzz-saw kind of activity. The blade is sharp and one cannot know on which side, left or right, it will cut its deepest niche. Are you ready for this kind of time?

This is the time of invention, a time to pioneer; a friend can come to your aid and transform dreams into realities. *But you have to have a dream in the first place.* Now you know whether this strikes that necessary responsive chord. To hear the sound you must have the dream. If you don't have the dream, ignore number 11 time. If you don't know what is meant by the dream, turn your Thought Dial away from 11. But if you do, if the dream is luminous, shining, paramount in importance, compulsive, consuming, then place your Thought Dial on 11.

If you play games, if the dream is absent but the dial

remains on 11, you will find yourself bogged down with detail, debt and confusion. Play games at your own risk! The subconscious, as I said earlier, doesn't have a sense of humor. *It takes direction from you—literally.* If you try to fool it you succeed only in deceiving yourself. Number 11 time is special, unique, demanding. Leave it alone if you are not ready.

DURING THIS TIME YOUR INTUITIVE INTELLECT IS HONED TO RAZOR-SHARPNESS. You act on first impressions. You have *implicit* trust in your "flash judgment." Does this frighten you? If so, turn the dial away from 11. But if the chord of recognition sounds, this *is* your time.

This is a time of *inspiration.* You are inspired enough to turn a dream into something solid. Your ESP comes to the fore; you trust first impressions and prove it by acting on them.

You deal with the *unseen.* You have a goal that cannot be clearly defined. But you know it is there and you are committed to reaching it. You teach, you inspire, you instill enthusiasm in others; there is a psychic income connected with this time, a *satisfaction* that may or may not translate into material gain. Plainly, you must be willing to sacrifice as well as to garner reward.

During this period you learn to be surrounded by people wishing to know; some are skeptical, some are faithful, some are superficial, some are dedicated. How many of the latter result from your efforts depends upon whether this truly is your time.

If concerned with a *theological* dilemma, dial 11. If concerned with spiritual knowledge, dial 11. If demanding answers from within, dial 11.

If it is something concrete you want—including cash on the line—ignore 11. Number 11 time demands the discipline of your faith. If you are lacking this, avoid trouble by turning *away* from 11.

You are, during this time, creative, sensitive, able to perceive when something of importance is about to occur. You size people up; many claim that you see through them. It is a fact that you can tell when an individual is sincere, when he is merely guessing, or when he is rationalizing.

During this time you promote original, inspirational projects. You build an organization, enhance its income potential. But the key note here is *potential.* You don't promote immediate cash, you don't turn the red ink into black at one stroke. You build, inspire, transform. You take time because you sense a dramatic change, a break from what was, you *know* what is to be.

When you dial 11 you are concerned with cycles, with time, with astrology, with divinatory arts. You want to correlate mundane happenings with planetary patterns, to find out how people respond to numbers. You study palms and relate the size and shapes of hands to human character. That's the kind of time this number 11 represents, and your subconscious will follow through if you so computerize it.

Do you want to teach? Dial 11. Do you want to inspire others to delve beyond material indications? Dial 11. But if you want merely to cash in, to serve as a back-fence guru, turn away from 11.

Are you concerned with psychology, religious writing, the mastering of arcane subjects? Dial 11. Do you want to write about astrology, teach it, appear on its behalf? Dial 11.

YOU LEARN BY TEACHING DURING THIS TIME. YOU GAIN BY SHARING KNOWLEDGE. But you don't share the traditional, you don't teach according to the traditional book. Instead, there are innovations, departures from the norm: the statistics are shaken, the museums rattle, the electricity is charged and the magnetism is strong. That's the kind of time you dial when you are on the 11 wave length.

You carry with you a *revelation* during this time. You want others to comprehend, to know and understand. You are asking, when you dial 11, for a time in which you can expose truth, bring to light new knowledge. This is a time of salvation, for uplifting thoughts, motives. You will battle for what you know to be right. Since this does not make it easy, you should stay away from 11 if you seek ease.

You have the devotion of a martyr during this time. Is that what you want? Does the chord of recognition sound loud and clear? If so, dial 11. Otherwise, get off this time period.

Are you preparing a unique television format, are you willing to stick by your guns? Dial 11. Do you want to preach, to save, to elevate, to uplift? Dial 11. Do you want to be accepted in an orthodox sense? Then get *off* 11.

Dialing 11 will make you unorthodox. Dialing this time brings a period of the unusual, makes you appear "far out," causes some to term you eccentric and worse. Can you take it? Are you dedicated, strong in beliefs, sure that what you have to offer as a message is worth reading? If so, dial 11. If not, find another time.

When you dial 11 you are unique, different, special in that you don't appear to have the usual motives or drives. Instead, you strive for a spiritual goal; you gain through teaching of a kind of hermetic knowledge. If you are weary of the usual routine, if you desire the flash of suddenness, then dial 11. IF YOU HAVE GONE THROUGH A DIVORCE, dial 11 to become acclimated.

If you have just purchased a house, just married, just settled down, leave 11 alone. When you dial 11 your subconscious draws to you conditions of break, divorce, quick change, erratic action. Dial 11 only when you are so dedicated to an ideal that the routine means nothing, the security can go by the wayside. You have to have the courage of your convictions, and the overwhelming desire to share those convictions.

Your friends now come from a different area. You are inventive and the people you attract are sympathetic toward those inventions. An electric charge permeates your actions. This is no time for the fearful, the timid, people afraid of shock. This is being made clear so that you don't dial 11 in expectation of being taken aboard a magic carpet. First you have to *create* that magic, to study it, understand it, become familiar enough with it so that you are at ease with it. If you are frightened, surprised, you will cause yourself unnecessary problems. This is no time for the person who wants to continue along with an ordinary path. IF YOU ARE A TEACHER WITH A NEW METHOD THAT BURNS WITHIN AND DEMANDS TO BE SHARED, then, and only then, must you dial 11. Otherwise, you only fail to teach that particular lesson, but you lose the opportunity to teach at all.

You *guide* others during this time and brighten your own inner light. You perceive, know, understand, possess the wisdom to bear with what could become ridicule. Obstacles become challenges, opposition serves only to strengthen your convictions, when you are truly on the 11 wave length.

DIAL 11 FOR A SPECIAL MISSION.

DIAL 11 FOR STUDIES CONNECTED WITH THE THOUGHT DIAL, ASTROLOGY, NUMEROLOGY.

DIAL 11 FOR UNIQUE METHODS OF TEACHING.

DIAL 11 FOR THE INSPIRATION WITH WHICH TO INSPIRE OTHERS.

DIAL 11 FOR ACTIVITY CONNECTED WITH THE UNORTHODOX, INCLUDING RELIGION.

DIAL 11 FOR INTEREST IN PSYCHIC AFFAIRS, IN ESP, IN TELEPATHY, IN BORDERLINE SUBJECTS, THOSE BETWEEN ACCEPTANCE AND REJECTION.

Are you determined that something worth studying, *knowing*, exists beyond known horzions? Then dial 11.

Number Twenty-Two Time

Number 22 time is when you tear down in order to rebuild. It is a time when you become the master of your own fate. You control circumstances rather than bow to them. Number 22 is associated with Pluto, the planet related to Scorpio, the Eighth House. Thus when you dial 22 you are getting accounts in order, probing the occult or hidden, agreeing with your mate on financial affairs; and you are conditioning your subconscious to rise above petty details and view the master building project. Dialing 22 brings you in contact with persons born under Scorpio, from October 22 to November 21.

Number 22 time promotes building, creativity. You lay plans, bring visions down to earth and inspire others to rise above their environment. You are unwilling to accept the status quo. The sky is the limit during this time. But with this heady atmosphere you also attract responsibility. People tend to accept you as the authority. Thus they believe in you, have faith in your beliefs, decisions. Knowing this creates a strain. Don't dial 22 if you don't want to be caught up in a cause. This kind of time causes you to investigate, involves you with the opposite sex, brings you in contact with subjects considered taboo.

Do you want to throw off feelings of insecurity? Then dial 22. Do you want to throw off fear caused by tradition? Then dial 22. Do you want to rebuild, create, leave a mark of individuality? Then dial 22.

When you dial 22 you often find yourself cast in a lonely sea. You learn to be self-reliant. There is a loss represented by one who took care of you, but allowed you little freedom. Number 22 time grants freedom but takes away the security blanket. If you're ready for this, dial 22.

Now you build. You do not get bogged down with details. You avoid the petty, the inconsequential. YOU SEE PROJECTS AS A WHOLE.

Money comes from people willing to invest in your grand vision. You lose if you are doubtful, fretful, tangled in a maze of red tape. IT IS WHEN YOU WANT TO RID YOURSELF OF DELAY AS A COMPANION THAT YOU DIAL THIS TIME.

This is a time for architecture. You streamline, you progress, you clear away debris, you delegate the small duties and assume the large role.

As stated in SUBCONSCIOUS THOUGHTS, this is *not* the time for false claims or false pride. This *is* the time to PRODUCE. Money will be forthcoming, perhaps from business or marital partners, from those who are inspired by your FAITH and BELIEF.

You dial 22 when ready to eliminate pettiness, inefficiency—both in business and personal life. You dial this time when ready to act—and react—on a grand scale. There is nothing halfway here; it is all the way. You commit yourself to a program. You program your subconscious to respond to challenge, to design, build, to envision, to see the whole rather than bits and pieces. This doesn't necessarily make you popular but it does get you attention. Many may not agree, but few can ignore you. Is this the kind of time you seek? Then dial 22.

You organize and reorganize. You convince others that you have the capabilities of turning loss to profit, defeat into victory. You would turn the Thought Dial to 22 when embarking upon a mission that will change the policy of an organization, would transform the individual or corporate image from that of smallness to one of grand design.

You dial 22 for a time when your sensitivity to the mood of the people is an asset. You put your finger on the pulse of the public. You highlight your ambition; you overcome obstacles; you hurdle challenges; you attract to you a dedicated group.

When you desire greater recognition, dial 22. When you want the opportunity to carry out ideals, dial 22. Leave this time alone, however, if you are motivated by envy, petty jealousy, resentment. Dial 22 only when you feel ready to carry a burden, to overcome handicaps. Number 22 does not automatically remove barriers. Number 22 does, however, condition you to take the reins, to speak up, to outline programs, to create formats, to delve into areas previously ignored, either out of ignorance or fear. Number 22 sets you down in the middle of an unexplored area. Your discoveries depend upon your present state of emotional-mental development. Number 22 time, along with 11 time, creates pressures. IT IS NO TIME FOR THE TIMID, THE FEARFUL, THE PERSON WHO WANTS SECURITY ABOVE ALL ELSE. BUT IT IS A TIME FOR THE PERSON WHO STRIVES, IS IMMUNE TO RIDICULE, IS WILLING TO BREAK WITH THE ESTABLISHMENT IN ORDER TO CREATE HIS OWN CLIMATE OF CREATIVE ACCOMPLISHMENTS.

Dial 22 specifically for dealings with financial organizations; for stock-market perception. The mood of the masses becomes a language you can understand during this time. Dial 22 specifically for dealing with secrets, taboos, mysteries, the occult, for extensive investigation of the mystery of life—and death. Number 7 is the séance room and 22 transcends the physical trappings; it brings you in direct contact with the reason we are here, and where we may be going.

Number 22 time, similar to 8, is a power time; it is NOT a time for compromise. During this period you commit yourself. The course is set, the die is cast. You build, you move. If there is a block, an obstacle, you build around it, but you build. Naturally, this time requires an expenditure of energy, confidence and dedication. And if that's what you are determined to have, dial 22. Otherwise, go back to the charted path, the safe course—and leave 22 alone.

This kind of time transforms dreams into realities, puts them to practical use. The 22 time, however, is for humanity at large. You move large groups, you perform actions for the benefit of many rather than for personal aggrandizement.

You are not thwarted during this time. You stand as a symbol; you inspire, captivate, supply the drive and the power. Does the chord of recognition strike? If not, get away from 22. If it does, you are ready to assume leadership, to sacrifice personal comforts for the greater good. If it is recognition without sacrifice you desire, you are on the wrong wave length. If it is power without responsibility, you also are wrong. But if it is the building of an ideal that you sincerely desire, you are right in placing the Thought Dial on 22.

Dial 22 when the drive, the inner voice, *demands* that you shake off lethargy in order to accomplish objectives in a large, meaningful sense. Dial 22 when the dynamics of your personal makeup propel you to the point of leadership. Dial 22 when you are ready to assume the role of spokesman or organizer; when you are ready to shake precedent, rattle orthodoxy, battle roadblocks to progress.

This is a time for launching huge projects. You direct energy along constructive channels. You are indignant at conditions that cause others to be exploited. You set an example, find the words, do the right thing at the right time. You attract creative, dedicated people, but you must avoid fanatics. Your judgment becomes your ally. You overcome temptation to surround yourself with protective coloring. You expose your aims, your motives. You are there for all to see and hear. You "find" yourself.

Do you want to bring order, evolve a system of making ideas working tools? Do you want that invention, thought, idea, to be more than a gleam in your eye? Dial 22.

In relations with the opposite sex, 22 is virile and brings with it a time when your imprint is solid, your seed potent. Leave 22 alone if you are merely dabbling, toying, experimenting.

Number 22 time generates energy, overthrows, tears down and rebuilds. It is symbolic of the phoenix that rises from the ashes. It is rebirth, regeneration.

If, in physical relations with a loved one, you have suffered a waning of power—and you seek to remedy the condition, set your Thought Dial on 22. This programs the subconscious to take proper steps, to build, to strengthen mind and body to the point where potency replaces weakness, strength dominates uncertainty, confidence once more leads to sexual fulfillment.

You build on a solid foundation during this time, for the potential comes into view. You ignore the petty, the people of little faith; you inspire because you are, at last, assured of the final outcome.

MAKE DEPOSITS, build your bank account as well as spiritual resources. In this kind of time you work with ideals, but you do *not* leave reality behind. Number 22 is a higher octave of 4, just as 11 is an intensified, enlarged aspect of number 2. This being the case, 22 time demands of you a realization that the building requires a foundation, that the organization needs workers as well as chiefs, that the dream takes money if it is to be fulfilled. You *deposit* in the sense that you accumulate power. You *deposit* rather than squander. And this takes determination, will power, dedication of purpose. Number 22 time aids you in *discovering* the purpose. You find yourself, and this makes your purpose, *your reason for being,* easier to comprehend. Is this what you desire? Are you coming close to recognition of what this time signifies? If so, you may be ready for 22.

During this time you tap inner resources. You are tested but your own self-testing is more important. You are satisfied with nothing less than achievement. You don't want a stand-off, a draw, an even decision. You want to rise, to emerge victorious. This is not an easy time to describe. Nor is it an easy time to achieve, to live through, to fulfill. Compromise is out. Principles are your mainstay, your guiding point, your road map. Be sure you understand this before directing your subconscious along these lines. If you are not ready, chaos could result. You may battle and belittle yourself, denigrate your own talents to the point of impotence.

Now you have been told; the 22 time has been delineated. The rest is up to you.

Do you paint, have you been sculpturing, writing, composing? Are you aiming for a master work, or at least one that opens new paths of expression? Then dial 22.

Are you ready for a sweeping reorganization of your business, your life? Then dial 22.

Otherwise—leave it alone!

20

A New Dimension

We have spoken at some length about the importance of approaching the Thought Dial with subconscious thoughts and specific questions. During the years since *Thought Dial* was conceptualized, while the experience of thousands of people was studied, a new dimension has been added—a dimension that leads us to the interpretation of *direct* and *abstract* thoughts, ideas, and associations.

A close analogy would be the well-known word-association test, whereby an individual is given a word, such as "door," and asked to reel off a number of other words that come to mind when he thinks of "door." Our Thought Dial varies in that the subject looks at or thinks of a word, such as "love," and selects three numbers. The numbers are totaled and reduced to a single digit between 1 and 9, with the exceptions of 11 and 22, the only double numbers retained as final totals.

The implications here, the possibilities are limitless. We are able to probe the subconscious in connection with such *abstracts* as LOVE, HATE, BEAUTY, DESPAIR, and in association with such *specifics* as SEX, MONEY, WORK, MARRIAGE, MOTHER, FATHER, etc.

Here is a sample test I devised, which was actually applied to a patient by a practicing psychologist, and reportedly with great success. Subsequently, other professionals—psychiatrists and medical hypnotists—utilized similar tests with encouraging results.

The patient will be called Mr. X. No mention was made to him of an actual Thought Dial. He was told simply to look at the words given below, and to place three numbers beside each word. He was also instructed to first relax and to write down any three numbers (as a subject would do in the "Your Subconscious Thoughts" section).

150

Mr. X first wrote 9, 11, and 3, for a total of 23, or 5. He was then confronted with the following words:

SAFETY

SEX

LOVE

JEALOUSY

HEIGHT

INFERIORITY

HANDSOME

MONEY

WORK

GIRL

SISTER-IN-LAW

AMERICA

SELF-CONFIDENCE

CHILDREN

MATURITY

MARRIAGE

COUSIN

MOTHER

DOCTOR

Mr. X then proceeded to place three numbers beside each of the words, with this result and the following totals:

SAFETY: 10, 203, 1. (totals 214, or 7)

SEX: 701, 12, 19. (totals 732, or 3)

LOVE: 21, 17, 23. (totals 61, or 7)

JEALOUSY: 26, 32, 35. (totals 93, or 3)

HEIGHT: 6, 11, 4. (totals 21, or 3)

INFERIORITY: 3, 7, 11. (totals 21, or 3)

HANDSOME: 22, 6, 36. (totals 64, or 1)

MONEY: 27, 32, 712. (totals 771, or 6)

WORK: 420, 56, 80. (totals 556, or 7)

GIRL: 19, 24, 20. (totals 63, or 9)

SISTER-IN-LAW: 40, 47, 50. (totals 137, or 11)

AMERICA: 71, 82, 95. (totals 248, or 5)

SELF-CONFIDENCE: 200, 4, 80. (totals 284, or 5)

CHILDREN: 2, 4, 7. (totals 13, or 4)

MATURITY: 31, 38, 20. (totals 89, or 8)

MARRIAGE: 10, 87, 23. (totals 120, or 3)

COUSIN: 30, 29, 17. (totals 76, or 4)

MOTHER: 58, 48, 39. (totals 145, or 1)

DOCTOR: 56, 48, 39. (totals 143, or 8)

It must be remembered that the subject, in this example, was *not* dialing, but merely giving spontaneous numbers in connection with the words in question. The subject had no idea what the test would reveal. The actual Thought Dial could just as well be used, but since a doctor was conducting the test, it was felt the atmosphere should be kept "clinical," that a Thought Dial might arouse suspicion, fear, or even worse, boil up academic prejudice within the patient. Use of it would have eliminated the large double and triple numbers, thus simplifying the process of addition, if nothing else. However, what counts is the end result, the totals, not by which method the totals were forthcoming.

Now, if we will but think, the enormous potential of such a process becomes evident. Here, the analyst is able to by-pass the conscious mind and *probe the subconscious* in connection with such factors as INFERIORITY, JEALOUSY, SEX and so on.

Let us now examine our subject's totals and draw some conclusions *based on the principles of Thought Dial*. First, his three numbers, given without reference to a word—9, 11, 3 (totals 23, or 5)—tell us he is (refer to number 5 in "Your Subconscious Thoughts" and other sections) concerned with relations with members of the opposite sex, with the possibility of marriage, with self-expression, with creativity; he wants to give of himself, make his mark, he is bursting with efforts toward self-expression. That is a beginning. It represents what is of concern to the subject. Here we are on "traditional" ground, or ground that is familiar. It provides a starting point. We are not elaborating: the student who has come this far is able to grasp principles. So, let us now see what our subject reveals when he places numbers beside the word "Sex."

The 3 total, as our lessons in the first edition have taught us, represents a scattering of forces, confusion—nothing certain here. Sex, for our subject, equals 3, giving light to a basic attitude of general confusion and anticipation. We note, also, that JEALOUSY totals 3.

Now we are once more *grasping principles*. Through our technique we are discovering *subconscious associations* in connection with our subject. We know that sex, for him, is 3: we have also discerned that jealousy similarly totals 3. Jealousy and sex are tied tightly together in his subconscious thoughts, though he *may not consciously* admit or even be aware of this fact.

Other 3 totals include HEIGHT, INFERIORITY and MAR-RIAGE. In all, under the 3 total we have SEX, JEALOUSY, HEIGHT, INFERIORITY and MARRIAGE.

These have been numerically or mathematically *grouped* through our Thought Dial technique and thus we have entered a *new psychological dimension*. We have by-passed hypnosis and endless hours of questioning and endless statistical applications. This is not, repeat *not,* to advocate that statistical application or hypnosis or more orthodox forms be eliminated—what we *are* offering represents *an added psychological tool* to be utilized in conjunction with other techniques if it is deemed necessary.

We now know that for our subject there is a *subconscious mathematical* grouping of HEIGHT, INFERIORITY, SEX, JEALOUSY and MARRIAGE. His symbol for this grouping is 3, representing basic insecurity, just as 3 itself is indicative of forces scattered, questions asked, general flurries of confusion.

GIRL, for our subject, totals 9, the symbol (check "What the Numbers Symbolize") of completion. *No other word carries this total for our subject.* His subconscious here provides us with one of his basic goals, as indicated by his initial total of 5. In attempting to achieve his goal, he has created a wall of obstacles based on a general feeling of inferiority and frustration, as indicated by the 3 total groupings.

His 5 subconscious indicator tells us, initially, what he needs, desires, attempts, wants—but this goal (conceivably—even very likely—marriage) is obscured by the fact that marriage is colored (for him) with CONFUSION (3), and this confusion applies to his other 3 groupings; that is, not only marriage itself, but sex, inferiority in connection with height and jealousy.

What we want to know is, what represents self-confidence for our subject—and he gives us a psychological clue through his total of 5 for SELF-CONFIDENCE, which is the same as his initial, or subconscious thoughts, total. This number, we already know, has to do with sex, just as the number 8 does.

What do we find when we look for 5 or 8 totals? Under 5, we have his general subconscious total, and we also have AMERICA and SELF-CONFIDENCE. We now know that our subject associates being in AMERICA, with SELF-CONFIDENCE.

The need for love is evident, and LOVE, for our subject, presents a problem similar to marriage, in that his total is 7, showing another kind of confusion—self-deception. Other 7 totals include SAFETY and WORK.

Our subject is telling us *through his subconscious,* that he will feel economically SAFE when he finds the "right" WORK and this will automatically result in the finding of LOVE. Love will bring him what he basically seeks: a home. The classical symbol for home is 6. For our subject, MONEY is symbolized by that total. He is telling us a story so startlingly clear!

It should be most definitely noted that the words given in this test are not arbitrary. Students and psychologists are urged to suggest other word lists, eliminating some, adding others, always varying to an extent—depending upon the subject or the patient and his problems as he states them, or as indicated through other techniques, either horoscopic or via orthodox procedures.

It is now time to have a look at the external Mr. X. Age: 32. Born in Czechoslovakia. Taken to Germany and placed in a concentration camp, May, 1944. Permitted to come to America in December, 1946. Feels he is "too short." Has inferiority about his "lack of height." Is concerned about the "right kind of girl" for himself. Concerned also about the "right job."

These external, or "conscious," revelations were most clearly perceived through use of Thought Dial technique.

Remember: this was not a postmortem—our factors were given BEFORE Mr. X's case history was made known!

We never saw him, so we had no idea about his HEIGHT, but through his number groupings he told us: INFERIORITY and HEIGHT, as well as SEX, JEALOUSY, MARRIAGE.

The psychologist treating Mr. X was able to provide immeasurable aid through this Thought Dial test. It is only the beginning of what the author positively believes will prove a boon, both to practitioner and patient.

Where we go from here—and how far—depends upon further experiment by *others,* by laymen, and by qualified persons in a variety of fields.

The practitioner can help the patient to recognize what is buried in his subconscious, can provide corrective therapy once the patient is able to *mathematically recognize* some of his innermost conflicts.

We have provided one example, admittedly incomplete, for the potential goes beyond our present knowledge. There were other experiments with similarly encouraging results. Our technique, in this case, was able to reveal WHY Mr. X showed decided tendencies to withdraw, to indulge in self-doubt and pity, as well as abuse at the hands of others. He was lethargic and felt he wasn't "good enough."

Thought Dial helped us and him to understand the *why* of these feelings of insecurity and confusion with regard to his basic wants, needs, desires, wishes, hopes, dreams, ambitions.

I leave it to other students and experiments to determine further conclusions, such as the grouping of DOCTOR and MATURITY (8). We also have COUSIN and CHILDREN (4). MOTHER is 1. SISTER-IN-LAW provides the only double number, 11.

This *new dimension* can and should be used in conjunction with other sections.

For astrological students, Mr. X's birth date: September 15, 1926, hour unknown. City and state unknown. Country: Czechoslovakia.

As an individual's life changes, so do his opinions, prejudices, inclinations, desires—and *thoughts*. Some persons are basically mature when it comes to ideas concerning such abstracts as LOVE or SUCCESS, while others display marked infantile tendencies. Use of the Thought Dial helps us obtain clear insight into what might otherwise remain vague abstractions.

Let us take, as our first example, the word "love." The subject is told to think of it and dial or instantaneously select three numbers, which are added in the usual way, until a single number between 1 and 9 is left, the only double numbers retained being 11 and 22. Incidentally, by "instantaneous" we do not necessarily mean "speedy." The time taken to select the numbers will vary with the individual. Some persons are able to dial the numbers quickly; others choose with what might be termed "deliberate speed."

Experiments conducted recently tend to indicate that THE MORE MATURE THE INDIVIDUAL . . . the more likely he is to dial or select numbers that total 6 when it comes to the word "love."

It might be fitting to close this chapter by sharing what could be called a "new dimension of the new dimension." To simplify matters, this breaks down to an example of one case in which the principles of the "new dimension" were untilized with apparent success.

I present this example so that serious students, including professional psychologists with intellectual curiosity, can observe the Thought Dial at work. This is what I call the Thought Dial Analytical Technique. I am convinced it is valid and important. I am further convinced that persons better trained than myself, in more orthodox psychological disciplines, should not delay one more second in familiarizing themselves with the Thought Dial.

Here, then, is an example of the Thought Dial Analytical Technique: *Subject is concerned with inability to sleep without aid of drugs.*

A study of our previous chapter on this technique makes it clear that we first provide the subject with words and ask for three numbers in association with each word. We utilize our own judgment in selecting the words. In this case we chose the following words. The subject provided the following numbers, which we added and reduced to single numbers.

SLEEP $= 473 = 14 = 1+4 = 5$
WORK $= 534 = 12 = 1+2 = 3$
FAMILY $= 693 = 18 = 1+8 = 9$
REST $= 224 = 8$
IRRITATION $= 893 = 20 = 2+0 = 2$
MOTHER $= 652 = 13 = 1+3 = 4$
FATHER $= 666 = 18 = 1+8 = 9$
BROTHER $= 341 = 8$
SISTER $= 295 = 16 = 1+6 = 7$
FOOD $= 347 = 14 = 1+4 = 5$
SEX $= 518 = 14 = 1+4 = 5$
HUSBAND $= 492 = 15 = 1+5 = 6$
BEAUTY $= 569 = 20 = 2+0 = 2$
SECURITY $= 646 = 16 = 1+6 = 7$
MONEY $= 888 = 24 = 2+4 = 6$
TIRED $= 421 = 7$
PENIS $= 691 = 16 = 1+6 = 7$
VAGINA $= 121 = 4$
CLITORIS $= 291 = 12 = 1+2 = 3$
ORGASM $= 689 = 23 = 2+3 = 5$
FULFILLMENT $= 691 = 16 = 1+6 = 7$

MARRIAGE $= 666 = 18 = 1+8 = 9$
HOME $= 691 = 16 = 1+6 = 7$
TENSION $= 931 = 13 = 1+3 = 4$
LOSS $= 421 = 7$
TROUBLE $= 333 = 9$
SUFFERING $= 431 = 8$
BED $= 218 = 11$
AWAKE $= 918 = 18 = 1+8 = 9$
BRIGHT $= 614 = 11$
HAPPY $= 361 = 10 = 1+0 = 1$
RELAXATION $= 691 = 16 = 1+6 = 7$
DREAM $= 341 = 8$
PAIN $= 893 = 20 = 2+0 = 2$
JOY $= 365 = 14 = 1+4 = 5$
APPLAUSE $= 641 = 11$
PROBLEM $= 641 = 11$
AGE $= 491 = 14 = 1+4 = 5$
REFRESHMENT $= 617 = 14 = 1+4 = 5$
IDEAL $= 696 = 21 = 2+1 = 3$
ENTHUSIASM $= 364 = 13 = 4$

Let me again make it clear that, after hearing about a woman's insomnia, I chose words, and the subject related three spontaneous numbers after each word. Now the job was to analyze the numerical (subconscious) symbols connected with those word-thoughts in an attempt to help with the problem. Here are my conclusions, which could serve as an example and help you in applying this new dimension.

In attempting to probe the subconscious, we first permit the symbol of SLEEP to come through, which it does as a total of 5.

This becomes our basis, or key. We know that anything added to the "ideal" that equals 8 will represent a key or fulfillment. Number 8 is power, and thus anything added to 5 that equals 8 will be significant. Anything added to SLEEP that equals 7 will be a root of the problem. Number 7 is indecision, doubt, as compared with the power-fulfillment of 8. SLEEP, according to the subject, is 5. That's the key. Any word that totals 3 makes SLEEP (added to 5) number 8 (power, achievement). Anything that totals 2 becomes 7 when added to the 5 of sleep, and represents the inner problem, the uncertainty, the core of trouble.

We are in deep water now and, although the technique

is relatively simple, I cannot lay it out in a perfect pattern for you. You will have to read these words over and over—and EXPERIMENT. Now, let's get on with this case history.

Key words that total 3 represent (3 added to 5 equals 8) areas or thoughts that add up to attaining the ideal (sleep). Words that the subject symbolizes, such as number 2 (2 added to 5 equals 7), would represent basic insecurities that compound the problem.

Number 5 itself is sleep, and the subconscious is able to associate some connections or associations with sleep itself. The subject thinks of sleep as 5, because she gives us the following numbers for SLEEP $(473 = 14 = 1 + 4 = 5)$. The following words also total 5 (sleep) for our subject: FOOD, SEX ORGASM, REFRESHMENT, JOY, AGE.

The subject, through the subconscious, tells us that sleep and joy are synonymous. So are sex and orgasm. So, too, are refreshment, food and age. The subject gives numbers for all these words that, when added, total 5—the same total as sleep, which the subject seeks without the aid of drugs.

In a very real sense the subject is revealing that, for her, sleep is associated with a kind of joyous security, physical (orgasm, refreshment, food) and ideal, which solves problems and replenishes mind and body. In her word groupings she includes age with number 5 (sleep, joy, orgasm, food, sex).

The word "irritation" totals 2 (when added to sleep-5 totals 7). Other 2 totals (sources or irritation or blocks to sleep) are BEAUTY, BED, BRIGHT, PAIN, APPLAUSE and PROBLEM. For this experiment, the 11 total is also regarded as 2 $(1 + 1 = 2)$.

The subject actually tells us here that often she is lying "on a bed of pain." Her need for BEAUTY and APPLAUSE are revealed as part of a PROBLEM.

Number 3, when added to 5-sleep, will give us some of the "strengths" the subconscious has stored, some of the ammunition to be utilized toward the attainment of peaceful, beneficial sleep. Of all the words, the subject totaled 3 for only two, those being IDEAL and CLITORIS.

The subject's "ideal" for producing what she lacks—ability to induce natural sleep—is complete and in independent control of her desires (clitoris). Subject's sleep problem, one can conclude, lies in the fact that she feels (subconsciously) that she should be in a vacuum, untouched by outward pressures and needs. The "ideal clitoris," which does not require a penis (which she totals 7—always the symbol of confusion, deception), is what subject may secretly desire in connection with her attitude toward sleep.

The subject's other problem, or 7, totals are the following: SECURITY, TIRED, FULFILLMENT, HOME, LOSS and RELAXATION. And, as mentioned, PENIS.

Subject's ability to attain fulfillment through drugless sleep is blocked by subconscious assaults of doubt (7) concerning security, by her battle to defeat a "tired" feeling, by her desire for *fulfillment,* which includes a home. She fears *loss* and lack of *relaxation.*

Subject associates TENSION with number 4, and groups this with MOTHER and ENTHUSIASM.

Subject's *tension* is related to efforts to please *mother* or to gain *enthusiasm* on part of one in authority.

Here one basic conflict is revealed. Subject's ideal for sleep is independence. But the need is for approval, even enthusiastic approval.

Subject gives 3 for *work,* thus grouping *work* with *clitoris* and *ideal.* Again, this would emphasize the need for a feeling of independence in order to bring about ideal conditions for drugless sleep.

Subject associates AWAKE with 9 and groups this with FATHER, FAMILY and MARRIAGE. Plainly, AWAKE finds subject aligned with allies (father, family, marriage mate). But ASLEEP finds disturbed areas, requirements, a need to be fulfilled through initiative and independence.

Those are my findings. Try for yourself. Have a person place three numbers beside words that you provide in connection with a specific problem. Study the example provided in the second section ("A New Dimension") and the example provided here. Then experiment, test and break through to your own dimensions.

Now, here are my basic conclusions and suggested therapy for this sleepless subject:

Subject should be given suggestion that in pleasing herself through independent action she is not necessarily alienating mother, authority, allies or security. Subject should repeat at sleep time:

I am free and independent, yet secure and protected. I am loved because I do love myself. I am entering a deep, refreshing sleep: sex and food are plentiful, available at my will. I am secure.

21

The Growth of
Thought Dial

The remarkable thing about *Thought Dial* concerns not only its reception by individuals, but the gratifying treatment received through the public communications media: newspapers, radio, television. Good reception in these areas helps the entire field of new thought, including astrology. This is no small matter. These areas have been, and still are, riddled with academic prejudice: doors are constantly closed and kept shut tight by the orthodoxy. When public opinion changes, only then will the power of the orthodoxy sway, at least a little, in favor of persons working on the "outside," persons interested in astrology, numerology, hand analysis, extrasensory perception, psychic phenomena, abstract science, etc. Academic prejudice is a very real threat: it spills over poisonous juices and attempts to destroy truth. Examination of numerous textbooks will readily show how this kind of poison has attempted to twist and alter history itself—i.e., Paracelsus *couldn't* have been an astrologer! Pythagoras didn't *really* believe in numerology; Nostradamus never really *used* astrology! Jung wasn't *serious* about astrology! No great astronomer *accepted* astrology! Mathematicians reject the *symbolism* of numbers! And on and on and on, *including dictionary definitions that are no longer definitions but editorial comments* ("astrology, a pseudoscience . . .").

But the pendulum is swinging over, slowly but surely. This publication, its reception, helps make that point clear.

Now, what are we basically stating? We are saying, with all the firmness at our command, that numbers are *subjective* as well as objective. We are saying that numbers have meaning and language and the power of communication, as alphabets do and as letters in alphabets possess that same power. We are declaring that numbers, like music, represent a *universal language*. We are saying that *thoughts*, intangible in themselves, can be reduced to number and thus made tangible.

True, the number is a symbol, not a literal statement. But to be able to obtain a *visual symbol* of such a thing as a *thought* is of paramount value, a giant step in progress, an exciting one, a tremendous adventure, the brink of enlightenment.

The actual *dial* of the Thought Dial is but a *mantram*, an instrument, just as the crystal ball is to the crystal-gazer or the bowl of water is to some clairvoyants. It would be just as practical, perhaps, for a person to name numbers or select them in any fashion, eliminating the dial. The dial is a convenience. It serves a purpose. But the experienced practitioner needn't be concerned with carrying a dial on his person. He can just as well have his subject write number selections or state them orally.

The principles, illustrations and examples as first espoused have held up. Experience is the one ingredient that improves the practitioner. *Use* of the Thought Dial is a necessity. Practice in *interpretation* of the numbers brings with it added skill. Just as an astrologer becomes skilled at interpreting planetary positions and aspects in a horoscope, so does the *user* of the Thought Dial gain added skill through numerous experiments. The basis, the principles, are there: how well they are *utilized* depends upon the determination and talent of the individual operator. A good analogy, of course, is the doctor who becomes an excellent diagnostician. The same symptoms are available to all doctors, but relatively few medical men become outstanding diagnosticians.

The fact that it *works* is the important factor. It works because of reasons outlined early in this book, or at least because of *some* of those reasons. All of the answers, as yet, are not known. To be successful in using the information contained here about *thoughts* and *numbers* it is important to *grasp basic meanings*. Afterward, the interpretations can be filled out, the "filling" process coming with practice, experiment, experience, skill.

Now, what is meant by the *grasping* of these meanings?

To date, the best example came from Dorothy Lyon of Los Angeles. She reports that "my first three trials gave me amazingly appropriate answers."

Miss Lyon puts it well: "appropriate answers." The Thought Dial takes the intangible or the unseen and permits us to "have a look," to examine something that contains substance and solidity (numbers). Miss Lyons tells of her first three trials. The initial one concerned retirement. Her total was 9.

The second was a question about a lady who felt she was not appreciated by her husband and wondered whether to leave him. The total was 4.

The third trial concerned a foot disorder. The total was 7.

I can recall, more than ten years ago, visiting Carl Payne Tobey, who was then confined to a hospital in New York. He was suffering a foot disorder. Carl gave three numbers. The total was 7. Number 7 is associated with Neptune. That planet is in turn related to the zodiacal sign of Pisces. That sign rules the feet. Number 7 is indeed "appropriate" in connection with Miss Lyon's third trial!

Number 7, of course, in another question or *thought*, might relate to an individual born under Pisces or its opposite sign, Virgo.

Just as the Twelve Houses of a horoscope conceivably could cover every department of life, so the number totals might be associated or analogous to any question or thought.

It might be well, at this point, to relate the totals to various bodily parts:

ONE—Back and Heart.
TWO—Stomach, Breasts.
THREE—Thighs.
FOUR—Heart, Back, Stomach.
FIVE—Arms, Hands, Kidneys.
SIX—Neck, Throat, Lumbar Regions.
SEVEN—Feet.
EIGHT—Knees.
NINE—Head, Face.
ELEVEN—Legs, Ankles, Teeth, Circulation.
TWENTY-TWO—Genitals.

In the first trial mentioned by Miss Lyon, the number 9 came up in a question relating to retirement. For a person who "grasps" the principles, this is an obvious total. Number 9, of course, relates, to finish, completion, the end of one phase of activity in preparation for another.

In her second example, Miss Lyon mentions the word "unappreciated" in connection with a woman who is pondering the state of her marriage. The total is 4. This is a natural total for such a thought or question, the number 4 being a symbol of restriction, of being "hemmed in" to a stifling degree. Number 4 brings a need for freedom or a feeling for freedom because, at least temporarily, it is being denied.

The Thought Dial consistently provides these "appropriate" symbols. It remains for each of us to strive for better understanding and interpretation of these totals. The sky is the limit with the principles we have evolved here.

Boxing promoter Tom Hurst, of Manchester, England, experienced success with the "Locating Lost Articles" section of *Thought Dial*. Surprisingly, so did numerous other persons. "Surprisingly," because this was one of the more speculative chapters. Mr. Hurst reports, "But the thing is amazing—even in little, silly things such as a length of sorbo rubber, ½ inches by ¼ inches and 8 feet long. It was looked for a dozen times. And more for a joke than anything, we tried the Dial. IN TWO MINUTES we had the rubber. . . ."

Mrs. Al Downs, of Los Angeles, received a telephone call from a friend in distress. She had lost something. Mrs. Downs asked her for three numbers. She then told her in which direction to look for the lost object. In a short time, the friend called again: she had found what she was looking for—and accused Mrs. Downs of being clairvoyant!

A professional astrologer in San Antonio, Texas, reports as follows: "I think I shall tell you at this point one of the main features in successful use of *Thought Dial*. It is this: I have a very good mail-order business, so I do this with each *unopened* (repeat, *unopened and unread!*) letter from a client: I place the letter (asking for astrological services) *behind* the *Thought Dial* (pressing against back of the Dial) then I concentrate. The result: practically *every* time (almost unfailingly) the subject's *birth sign* or *ascendant* is dialed!"

The above represents application of the theory that the

symbols are analogous or symbolic of the birth sign, as explained in the first edition, at the beginning of the section titled "Direct Questions Answered."

The communications media reception has been encouraging. Ben Hunter, of radio station KFI, Los Angeles, George Fisher, of KHJ, Los Angeles, and numerous others, including James Crenshaw, of the *Los Angeles Herald & Express* have reacted with favorable interest to the Thought Dial concept.

An unusual communication was received from Lucille Wallenborn, of Bell Gardens, California. She declared that *Thought Dial* seemed only to reiterate "the problem—or give a number which corresponds to what I am consciously thinking, hoping, or fearing." This woman, in other words, finds that the Thought Dial tells what is *consciously* on her mind, but does not probe deeper or provide special insight. In itself, this is interesting and certainly worthy of consideration. The theory behind the Thought Dial is that we are *aware* of the right answers, but very often those answers are buried deep in the subconscious, and if the answers are unpleasant, the censor, or conscious mind, is apt to distort them by the time they appear at the surface. Miss Wallenborn's experience seems to slightly contradict this theory, although her experience in general is an encouraging one for the student, for it provides fuel for thought and further experiment.

Kathleen F. Barnes, of Detroit, presents what she terms "certain startling facts regarding my experience with *Thought Dial.* ..." She had been a student of Carl Payne Tobey's course in astrology: it was through Tobey that she came into possession of it. She explains that she seems to have a natural distaste for mathematics, so it was with some surprise that she found herself investigating "certain strange designs involving digits and numbers." At first, she states, she was merely intrigued. But later, "I was engaged in a most diligent search for clues that would give this design some astrological meaning. Having found 'the key' I was off in search of 'the lock' to which it belonged. It turned out that 'the key' fit into an almost uncanny system of investigating the structure of a chart and the life belonging to it."

Miss Barnes goes on to report:

Naturally, this fascinated me, but because I was doubtful of my ability to get the idea across successfully to Mr. Tobey (it's hard to explain the details), I developed a strange impression of having a lion by the tail and did not dare to let go, so I merely continued to use the formula in experimenting with charts.

I am not a professional astrologer—at least not yet. Then Thought Dial arrived. At first I was disappointed, and then exceedingly annoyed with it because it seemed to clutter up my lovely number system. However, there was something about my annoyance which called for an explanation, and as is customary, when my mind goes wandering, something unusual turned up. Something about this Thought Dial produced a sense of familiarity. I set out to discover what it was, and holy! purple!! Shades of JUPITER!! it turns out that the system incorporated into Thought Dial paralleled my "mantric" number system, which is based emphatically on Mr. Tobey's planetary number assignment. They both operate by the same principle. Though it was a little difficult to track down this similarity . . . it eventually became obvious that the numbers assigned to houses and planets by Mr. Tobey were accurate and your interpretation, instead of upsetting them, merely proved their accuracy. Thought Dial becomes an expression of the dynamics stressed in any Natal or Solar chart PLUS the mathematical design of the transits.

Miss Barnes concludes by saying:

For me, this links Thought Dial with Mr. Tobey's work in a most harmonious way. By allowing for the changes effected by TIME and MOTION, the total and complete design is indicated by the Thought Dial. My "mantric system" has its source in incontrovertible facts. The cycles incorporated as parts of a design and "dialed" by the astrologer in sets of three total up to a whole number that explains the combined dynamics and, at the same time, highlights any particular aspect which contributes to the dynamic in motion.

The whole effect is somewhat uncanny because the

chart seems to live and breathe, and to tell you the truth, I felt a little bit afraid of it until I encountered Thought Dial *because it is a confirmation of the "mantric system" which was, to say the least, most electrifying.*

I acknowledge Thought Dial *as the "Geiger Counter" of the astrological realm.*

So, here we have an example of a student who had evolved her own numerical system combining it with principles of astrology, in this case Mr. Tobey's course. She states that her system "worked." Then, along came *Thought Dial* and her *own system* suddenly basked in the light of greater clarity.

At least two psychiatrists, one medical doctor who is not a psychiatrist, and one consulting psychologist, now make use of *Thought Dial* or apply its principles. These responses and results are provided because, though in themselves they may not prove or disprove a thing, the *combination* may help us toward greater understanding of what we have here, or toward eventual uses in specific areas of life. A little later, a new dimension of *Thought Dial* will be revealed. This dimension, it is felt, represents perhaps a new, important use. It is a psychological technique that the author staunchly believes will—in the not-too-distant future—be integrated into numerous areas of psychological testing.

For now, let us continue with reactions and responses, the reports of experiences encountered by users of *Thought Dial*. L. D. Wittkower, Sr., of Dallas, Texas, reports, "So far *Thought Dial* has proven so accurate it is amazing. I have never experienced anything like it."

John R. Hester, of Charlotte, North Carolina, comments, "I recently received my *Thought Dial* and it is literally *astounding!* It got me interested in numerology, which I find supplements my interest in astrology and the other esoteric branches. The horary astrology charts that I set up to seek answers to various questions used to keep me in a state of chronic frustration, due to the myriad varieties and necessity for skillful correlation of so many factors—a chart seldom gave a clear answer. *Thought Dial* has circumvented this in an indescribably satisfying way."

W. R. Timoney, of Pasadena, California, a valuable worker and contributor of findings to the Institute of Abstract Science, in Tucson, Arizona, states, "I get the impression ... that you lean on authority to too great an extent. It is when you get away from authorities that you are best. One of the best uses of external evidence you make in the entire book is the section 'Picking Winners.' You quote Matt Weinstock, of the *Los Angeles Mirror News*, to give some details. You fill in with some more details. You describe Ben Hunter's experiment, the outcome, and you analyze the procedure. This is first rate, scientific reportage. But in many places you try to tie astrology and the Thought Dial together. Maybe they are a part of the same whole; maybe not. Your arguments are not convincing. The Thought Dial is a very personal thing. It is analogous to a telephone line between the conscious and subconscious. Astrology is somewhat impersonal. It is analogous to a weather map of conditions surrounding the entire mind—conscious, subconscious, censor, etc. Because you use the symbols of astrology, you should not conclude that you use the principles. That may or may not be so. I happen to think you are much closer to the truth when you consider the Thought Dial as some kind of mantram."

Robert J. Trolan, of Indianapolis, Indiana, who is a "name analyst" and "Tarotologist," dispatches lengthy communication which, though on the whole disparages Thought Dial, also contains much thought. Mr. Trolan opens by stating he pursued Thought Dial with an open mind and avid interest. "I experimented with it and gave it a good deal of thought for about eight hours. My wife, who also knows a good deal about the 'Tarot' through 15 years of association with me and my work, also examined your work quite closely! Upon both completing our checking of same, we were of virtually the same opinion, 'It is a marvelous idea and shows real ingenuity!' However, we also agreed that the last word, 'Ingenuity,' is exactly the only fault we both could find with *Thought Dial*.

" 'Ingenuity' is generally defined as (1) Cleverness in inventing; ingeniousness; (2) cleverness of design or construction; as ingenuity of plot; with syn.—Inventiveness and Originality."

Mr. Trolan goes on to explain his reaction: "We believe that, like hundreds of other authors we have read and, with a few exceptions, like so many modern and 'so-called experts' on symbology, both yourself and Mr. Tobey have succumbed to the same error that has plagued both our esoteric and exoteric sciences for the last several thousands of years! That is to inject their own 'ingenuity, cleverness, and inventiveness,' to take, as it were 'fallacious license' with the symbology handed down to us by our mentors and superiors, the most ancient of 'Ancients.' The most astounding lack of disparity noticed in your work, is your almost studious avoidance of mention of the 'Sacred Tarot of Egypt,' or mention of men like Eliphas Levi, Elbert Benjamine (C.C. Zain), Max Heindel, John H. Dequer, and the sincere, but incomplete St. Germain."

Mr. Trolan explains why, although he agrees with some of the text comprising the first edition, he disagrees with other facets of *Thought Dial*. He then closes by stating, "In closing, may I please again compliment you on your extraordinary accomplishment and upon the fact that your basic idea is sound. My only regret is that you could have the temerity to tamper with ... mathematical verities and immutable certainties, just as Pythagoras did long before you, thereby coming up with a hybrid thing called numerology, which is here and there correct and mostly horribly incorrect. I am glad I have *Thought Dial*, as it is of great interest to me, although it only serves to prove either how right you are and how wrong I am ... or vice-versa."

From Josephine L. Whitbeck, of St. Helena, California, this communication: "My neighbor, Gordon Jackson, lent me his *Thought Dial*. When I had read enough to see what it was about, I tried the 'Your Subconscious Thoughts' section, came out with a 6, and some advice on a problem of long standing, which applied very well. Then I tried the 'Yes and No Technique' with the question 'Shall I buy a *Thought Dial*?' Total was 1 (Yes-Definite). This pleased me. If it had been No, I think I would have got one anyway ..."

I want to take this opportunity to call attention to wonderful reaction and cooperation from one in the academic world. He is Dr. Hugo Norden, professor of the Theory of Music at Boston University. After receiving his copy of *Thought Dial*, Dr. Norden began a correspondence with the author which, ultimately, will benefit all. Dr. Norden, on September 9, 1958, wrote:

"I have been spending some time with your *Thought Dial* and the accompanying book. Your mention of the possibilities of subconscious use of numbers interests me. Some musical works by Bach come to mind:

Passacaglia in C minor—21 sections, but so arranged as to bring in 4 overlapping 11-section units.
Sinfonia No. 1—21-measure form, featuring 9 in a great many ways.
Sinfonia No. 3—25-measure form, featuring 4 overlapping 7-measure units.

"This list could, of course, be continued indefinitely. But these three show a system.

"Now comes the question that every student asks: Is this organization of ideas deliberate or does it 'just happen'? Personally, I am inclined to believe it was conscious up to a point, but that at a point that *cannot* be determined by analysis, the mechanism took over and developed features that were never planned nor intended by the composer."

Dr. Norden goes on to say: "In my work I have gradually become aware of something that is undoubtedly 'old stuff' to you; namely, that numbers operate in two ways: (1) as organizational numbers, as in the Bach Sinfonia No. 1 where the 21-measure form is divided into 13 plus 8 measures by a very conspicuous division, and (2) as 'essence' numbers arising out of the organization numbers, as in the case of 9 functioning within the 8:13:21 form. Curiously enough, 7, 9, and 11 are most often 'essence' numbers, and not often organizational numbers."

In reply to Dr. Norden's comments, the following note was sent by the author, reproduced here for possible use or comment by the reader:

I agree emphatically that certain stages or phases are "planned" and after that the subconscious takes over and the organizational numbers take a back seat to what you term the "essence" numbers.

Numbers, of course, are interchangeable with letters: the vowels are "essence" or emotional while the consonants are apt to be organizational or utilitarian.

Here is an experiment I wish you would try: take a composition or work and think about it and then give three spontaneous numbers. Total the result. Think of how certain works would affect certain of your students. Put down the total you think would represent the student's attitude or thoughts toward that work or composition or composer. Then, actually ask the student to think and select the numbers. See how close you come to guessing his total. Or, see if his total does not reveal more to you about the particular student, or that work, than you previously knew. . . .

Dr. Norden is continuing to experiment and to contribute and to make valued suggestions.

Charles A. Jayne, Jr., chairman of Astrological Research Associates, New York, and editorial director of *In Search,* an international astrological quarterly, refers to *Thought Dial* as "amazing," and explains, "I say 'amazing' since only the night before last Dr. ———— sat in our living room and raved about it. He is a psychiatrist and has been testing *Thought Dial* for some time. He states that it is really uncanny. Please do not use his name. . . ."

The psychiatrist mentioned by Mr. Jayne is not the only one who is utilizing the principles of *Thought Dial* in his work.

Let me now quote from a letter by Harry Redl, a brilliant San Francisco photographer:

"I don't know too much about the principle of Thought Dial but it instantly reminded me of a method used by the late Dr. Wilhelm Stekel, of Vienna, who was a student of Freud along with Jung.

"Dr. Stekel, upon reaching an impasse with an inhibited patient, would ask the patient to *name any three numbers that came to his mind.*

"Stekel's interpretation of the numbers was based not on metaphysical or magical considerations, but rather on direct symbolism.

"As I recall, the number 1 would represent the penis, number 3 would symbolize the male genitals with testicles, while number 5 was the human hand, and so on.

"Dr. Stekel also requested, from his patient, the birth

dates of relatives, durations of relationships, and the age of the patient at the time of trauma occurrences. . . ."

Mention of Dr. Stekel's experiment is, without doubt, both interesting and exciting. It reveals, among other things, that others (or at least one outstanding psychiatrist) have *perceived* the possibility of using numbers to probe the secrets of the mind. Interestingly, Dr. Stekel (according to Redl) associates number 5 with the hands, which would be in complete harmony with the Thought Dial.

22

Conclusions

Admittedly, the title of this section is misleading. The late philosopher and psychologist William James once said, in effect, that nothing is concluded that we might conclude from it. In a sense, this is true when we talk about the Thought Dial. It is a start, a spark that could break out into a flame: the purpose of this work is to provide that spark. It will be up to readers, to students, to those who experiment with the material we have provided here—it will be those persons who kindle the spark and create, finally, a rousing flame, the warmth that comes with greater knowledge.

As I say, I know the Thought Dial "works." I have tried, in these pages, to tell all I *consciously* know of this *mantram*, this device which, at present, clearly falls into the field of the *mantic* sciences. There are really no conclusions possible at this time. But the necessity of putting down what we do know seemed imperative: what will come of it, as I say, remains to be seen.

I know that *disciplined experiment* is required: the Thought Dial, in the current stage, can be compared to Benjamin Franklin putting a kite aloft in an electric storm. In itself, that act was meaningless. What it meant to the future, of course, was quite another matter.

It is my hope that men of the caliber of Drs. Rhine and Jung, and others, will conduct experiments with the Thought Dial, aided by the experiences and reports of readers of this work. When we deal with the language of symbols we are on such fertile ground that no real end, or "conclusion" is in sight. There is so much to try, to do, to read, to conclude!

Anais Nin, the writer of superb novels, talks of the *need* for symbols. A listener asks, "Why not say what you mean in the first place and thus eliminate symbols?" She replies that often the "truth" is too terrible to bear, and only through the use of the symbol can the conscious mind comprehend what is buried deep, in the subconscious or secret or hidden mind.

She is borne out by others, in various fields of endeavor. Leo Stalnaker, in his excellent *Mystic Symbolism in Bible Numerals*,* declares: "The origin of the science of symbols is lost in the maze of early antiquity. Though the beginning is not known, it doubtless connects itself with the cradle of humanity, and the science comes down to us from an age when only a few could read or write. Man's earliest instruction was by symbols. A thing to be symbolic must really mean something, and must, in its nature, be a proper, adequate or fitting sign or token of something."

Stalnaker, like Lawrence Lipton, points out that "The importance of numerical symbolism to the ancient perhaps arose from the fact that the letters of the Hebrew language were originally numerals, and the entire Bible being composed of different groups or combinations of Hebrew letters, it came to be the common belief that the true meaning or proper interpretation of difficult passages of Scripture could best be ascertained or reached only by resorting to the numerical value of those letters."

Man's way of *communicating,* his language, his alphabet, the sounds and words he utters, are *symbols,* probably all relating to number. Through the use of the Thought Dial, the subconscious is able to communicate with our conscious minds, much in the manner that dream symbols can enlighten us. The literature available is enormous, from the Bible to the most modern scientific texts. I will

* C & R Anthony, Inc., Publishers, New York. 1956.

not—this, I admit might be an error—attempt to provide a list of recommended reading. I know I would, through ignorance or carelessness, neglect to mention pertinent material.

What I hope to do, from time to time, is to issue supplemental material to be utilized in connection with *Thought Dial*. The material will be based on future experience (experiment), both on a personal level and from reports obtained from readers—plus additional "reading" research.

Kurt Seligmann, in his remarkable *The History of Magic** (originally published under the title *The Mirror Magic*) states, "Without pretense to original scholarship, my investigation has been guided by such scholarly works as those of . . ."

In a way, that is what I wish to say: no pretense is being made that *Thought Dial* falls into the category of "scientific" or "scholarly" work. But I have been guided by the highest motives and by great works and scholars. If the reader was by my side, in my study, I would reel off a list of recommended reading. My "intuitive intellect" tells me it is not in place here, for the material ranges from the volumes of writers Henry Miller and Gertrude Stein, to those of Nostradamus, the interpreters of the *Kabala*, to the writings of Sepharial, Isidore Kozminsky, Seligmann, Jung, Cheiro, Evangeline Adams, Freud, Ariel Yvonne Taylor, Dr. Alexander Cannon, Florence Campbell, Stalnaker, Clifford Cheasley, Alfred Still, Clark E. Moustakas, Karen Horney, Constance Reid, Tobey, Grant Lewi, Manly Palmer Hall, Charles Fort, Rhine, William James, Marc Edmund Jones, Lilly, Ptolemy, Dr. Gustaf Stromberg, Mrs. L. Dow Balliett, Lawrence Lipton, Aldous Huxley, Waldo Frank, Julia Seaton. This list could be extended indefinitely, for it includes such sources as the Bible and the *Kabala* and the *Zohar* and so on, right up to the present: the language of *thought* and *symbol* is universal, a part of Nature, of life itself.

As I have said, before his death Thomas Alva Edison was reported to be engrossed in the possibility of a "telephone between worlds," a physical device which, he speculated, would eventually make it possible for persons living to communicate with those who had met bodily death. His

* Pantheon Books, New York, 1948.

theory, like the theories of Dr. Stromberg, Sir Oliver Lodge, Sir Arthur Conan Doyle and others, was that the human personality or memory or "spirit" survived after bodily death. There could be an analogy between Edison's "telephone between worlds" and the Thought Dial.

The subconscious, or "inner mind," may be in contact with whatever it is in man that survives. I do not know or claim to understand the subconscious. Like so many other things in our language, it represents a symbol—to me it is a convenient way of giving a "name" to the force that is tapped through utilization of the Thought Dial.

I defer my conclusion.

I await further word—from you.

Other SIGNET Books You Will Want to Read

☐ **UFO'S—THE WHOLE STORY by Coral and Jim Lorenzen.**
An overview of the UFO problem with a history of
recorded sightings and a look at the Condon Report.
(#Q5220—95¢)

☐ **THE BISHOP PIKE STORY by Allen Spraggett.** A pioneer
into the mysteries of parapsychology and the psychic
and close personal friend of Bishop Pike, has written
a fascinating biography of the life of the most prominent
and controversial religious figure of this decade.
(#Q4400—95¢)

☐ **INTIMATE CASEBOOK OF A HYPNOTIST by Arthur Ellen
with Dean Jennings.** One of America's leading hypnotists who has treated some 150,000 subjects, including
Tony Curtis, Maury Wills, George Shearing, Vic Damone
and many of lesser fame, presents here a compelling
account of hypnotism as a healing art. (#P3725—60¢)

☐ **FORTUNE IN YOUR HAND by Elizabeth Daniels Squire.**
An expert hand analyst and syndicated columnist provides a step-by-step illustrated "do-it-yourself" guide to
enable readers to gain insights into character and
personality through interpretation of signs in the hand.
(#T3448—75¢)

☐ **MANY MANSIONS by Gina Cerminara.** The most convincing proof of reincarnation and ESP ever gathered in
one volume. A trained psychologist's examination of the
files and case histories of Edgar Cayce, the greatest
psychic of our time. (#Q3307—95¢)

THE NEW AMERICAN LIBRARY, INC.,
P.O. Box 999, Bergenfield, New Jersey 07621

Please send me the SIGNET BOOKS I have checked above. I am
enclosing $_____(check or money order—no currency
or C.O.D.'s). Please include the list price plus 25¢ a copy to cover
handling and mailing costs. (Prices and numbers are subject to
change without notice.)

Name_____

Address_____

City_____State_____Zip Code_____
Allow at least 3 weeks for delivery

More SIGNET Books of Special Interest

☐ **TRUE EXPERIENCES WITH GHOSTS by Martin Ebon.**
In this anthology, fourteen instances of baffling super-
natural adventures are examined in the light of the new
science of parapsychology. (#T5348—75¢)

☐ **YOUR MYSTERIOUS POWERS OF ESP by Harold Sher-
man.** Extraordinary cases involving extrasensory perception and ways to release your own mysterious powers
of ESP are revealed. (#Q4841—95¢)

☐ **THE PSYCHIC WORLD OF PETER HURKOS by Norma
Lee Browning.** A professional skeptic, with the reputation for exposing frauds, proves beyond all reasonable
doubt that Peter Hurkos, a consultant on the Sharon
Tate and Boston Strangler killings, is a man with phe-
nomenal psychic powers and one of the greatest psy-
chics since Edgar Cayce. (#Y4779—$1.25)

☐ **THE TAROT REVEALED: A Modern Guide to Reading
The Tarot Cards by Eden Gray.** A fascinating and au-
thoritative introduction to the ancient art of the Tarot
cards. Special Feature: A special order blank is in the
book so that you can order an Albano-Waite Tarot Deck.
(#Y4078—$1.25)

☐ **THE UNEXPLAINED by Allen Spraggett.** A comprehen-
sive account of the most recent developments in parapsychology. Includes interviews with such well known
authorities as Jeane Dixon and Nandor Fodor.
(#Q3503—95¢)